THE GUIDE FOR PENNY STOCK INVESTING

2646-LOWY

THE GUIDE FOR PENNY STOCK INVESTING

Donny Lowy

To order additional copies of this book, contact:
Xlibris Corporation
1-888-7-XLIBRIS
www.Xlibris.com
Orders@Xlibris.com

CONTENTS

Welcome to the most comprehensive book on penny stock investing. The goal of this book is to supply the novice investor along with the experienced professional equity trader with all the information he or she will need to be educated in the realm of penny stock investing. This book can be used as an educational totem for those investors who were always curious about investing in penny stocks but did not know where to start. This book will guide the investor by explaining the various concepts and terms in an easy to understand language. Besides its usage as an instructional book for those who have never invested in a penny stock, this book will also serve as a manual for the veteran trader. As an investor you will be familiarized with all the concepts behind micro cap investing. You will learn what the difference between a reverse merger and a reverse split is. You will be presented with many new terms and concepts. Some of those terms will be familiar since they are used in connection with investing in the broader market while other terms will be specific to penny stocks. In addition to the various terms and concepts you will be able to benefit from another facet of this book.

You will be able to personally benefit by using this book as a manual on penny stock trading. This book will teach you proven strategies that work when it comes to penny stock investing. Instead of repeating shallow, but nice sounding ideas, the concept of buying low and sell high, you will be given substantial strategies that are extremely effective when done correctly. You will have at your disposal strategies that only experienced traders know. The strategies in this book have been collected from first hand experience and from the collective experience of numerous experienced penny stock investors.

We all know the frustration we encounter upon spending a few weeks reading a book on investing and then being left out to dry when we are dealing with a real life situation. After finishing the book we feel excited since we have just read 400 pages telling us that the key to investing is following a few simple ideas. All we will need to do is read the daily business newspaper. The investment mass media publications will have us believe that once we have written down their simple ideas and have a newspaper handy we will be on our way to making our first million in the market. Unfortunately this approach to investing is as far from the truth as possible. How many times have we read a strategy in an investment book only not to be able to apply it in the real world of trading? The reason that we often cannot apply the strategies we read in an investment book is that most of the strategies we see and hear on the evening news are based on theory and are not proven outside of the classroom. Many theories only work in a perfect world where the market always responds the way it is supposed to respond to an event. Among the popular misguided theories is to only look for companies with solid earnings. But reality has shown us that this theory does not hold its weight in the market. How many times has a company released positive earnings and still experienced a loss in its market value? On the other hand how many stocks continue escalating in value in light of the fact that they do not have any earnings? If you knew that a company was going to earn a billion dollars in six months would you let yourself be preoccupied with the fact that it is loosing money now? The simple fact is that there are many other investing rules which are more accurate than the frequently repeated advice we hear thrown out every day by analysts and the popular media. Next time you hear someone tell you that "all you need to do is buy a stock and hold it" ask him how long he plans on holding the next horse and buggy company. The point is that once a market for a product becomes eliminated then the companies involved in that segment will either have to change direction or will shortly be bankrupt. Now you might be wondering if there is a method altogether for investing or if you should just throw darts at the financial pages and see on which stocks the darts fall. Well, before you give up investing and head for the black jack tables read on. There is a method to the game. And the method consists of many smaller steps which when followed properly will lead on to successful investing. This book will provide you with the broader method and the small steps. If you follow the advice and stick to the enclosed discipline you will learn allot and might even become substantially rich from your investments.

Why penny stocks?

This book is focused on penny stocks. While there are many different types of investing one can partake of the author believes that micro cap investing is the most rewarding one. Micro cap investing has the potential to yield huge gains in short period of time. It is very common for penny stocks to move upwards of 25% in any given day. Keep in mind that the adverse means that they can also move down 25% on any given day. The nature of penny stocks makes them both very rewarding and very dangerous. Then why invest in them at all? Because in this world the more risk you take the more reward you are posed to gain. If you put your money in a bank account you will eliminate all risk short of a total banking melt down. You will always be able to access your money regardless of the general condition of the market. A bank account seems like the perfect type of investment vehicle until you realize that the interest you earn hardly keeps up with inflation after you have paid taxes. You can then choose to increase your tolerance of risk and invest in a bond with relative security and safety. You will then have peace of mind but also a very small return on your investment. If you decide that you are willing to risk your money you can enter the security arena via a mutual fund or the purchase of a security like General Motors and hope that by the end of the year your investment has grown by 20%. You have increased your risk and have increased your return potential at the same time. By investing in an established mutual fund or company you have both minimized your risk and potential at the same time.

But what if you wanted the opportunity to double or triple your money in a month? You would be hard pressed to find a stock trading on one of the larger exchanges that had the potential to double in a month. Now keep in mind that if a stock existed which had the potential to double in a month it would also have the potential to lose all of its value in a month. But what if you decided that knowing the huge risks you were about to undertake you still wanted a crack at buying stocks that could double your money in a month. You would find those stocks among the ranks of the penny stocks. These companies would be small companies with small operations but large aspirations. These companies would be driven by a dream and the necessary ambition to beat the odds. The odds would be stacked against them in many aspects. A majority of these companies will never progress beyond the development stage. But the slim percentage of companies that do beat the odds can experience dramatic growth in their stock prices of upwards of 10,000% in a year.

So is it worth investing in penny stocks? The answer is yes and no. You will have to look within yourself and discover if you have the ambition and persistence to learn everything there is about penny stocks. This book should prove to be more than enough ammunition to beat the odds and discover the right next penny stocks. But it is up to you to decide if you have the courage and ability to take the large risks associated with investing in them. Use this book as an educational manual, and make sure to consult a broker before making your decisions. This book is not meant to give advice, it is only written for educational purposes. Read the conclusion of the book before making any investment decisions. It is located at the end of the book. Good luck.

CHAPTER 1

What is a Penny Stock?

Before we can enter the penny stock arena we have to a clear grasp of what it is we are dealing with. We need to have a definition of what a penny stock is and where it trades. Without a basic definition of the stocks we will be investing in we will make countless mistakes out of confusion and lack of direction. Like any entrepreneur, an investor must know what the market they are entering is comprised of. She must research it fully and know all the details that pertain to the given business segment she is entering. Before she commits one dollar to her new pursuit she will make sure that she knows everything there is to know about her market cold. We will emulate the entrepreneur by learning everything there is to know about penny stocks and the market they trade in. In order to do so successfully we will analyze the penny stock market from the ground zero.

To start with we need to decide upon a definition of what a penny stock is. Some investors mistakenly assume that a penny stock is a stock that trades for a cent. While there are many stocks that trade for a cent and when traded correctly can yield vast profits, the definition is broader. Some investors consider any stock trading under $5 to be a penny stocks. Those investors seek to avoid stocks they deem to be highly risky. By labeling any stock trading under $5 a penny stock they help separate themselves from what they see as highly risky securities. While both definitions are accurate four our intents and purposes we will define a penny stock as any company trading on the over the counter market.

Our definition of a penny stock will eliminate stocks trading under a dollar on the New York Stock Exchange or stocks trading for
.50 on the Nasdaq Small Cap market. The reason we will not
consider those stocks to be penny stocks is because more often
than not a stock trading for under a dollar on one of the larger
exchanges will soon be delisted due to dire troubles in its business.
A stock trading under a dollar on a major exchange most likely
once traded way above that price and now due to either misman-
agement or external factors is in financial troubles and headed for
bankruptcy. While there is an art to investing in those companies
I have found that it is more profitable to invest in companies that
are still awaiting their future than companies which have already
experienced what the future holds for them and are now in decline.

The market cap is not relevant at this point. Later in the book
we will discuss how to use the market cap when deciding on a
stock. At this point our only definition of a penny stock is a stock
which trades either on the over the counter market or on the pink
sheets. You must be wondering why I would ignore the market
cap when defining a penny stock. There are many penny stocks
with share prices in the dollar range and a market cap of over a few
hundred million dollars, sometimes even equaling a mid cap in
the price of their market valuation. Clearly those companies should
not be considered penny stocks any longer? If they are worth more
money than an established company trading on the Nasdaq then
they really are not penny stocks any longer?

The answer depends on the company and on the market valuation for that type of business. We will discuss in a later chapter
how to understand and come up with a fair market cap for a company. But for now we will ignore the market cap and focus on the
market the stock trades on. The only other parameter we will use
to define a penny stock is that it must be trading under a dollar at
the point we buy it. We might chose to hold a stock as it climbs
above a $1 but we will never consider a stock over a $1 to be a
penny stock for our purposes.

CHAPTER 2

The OTC Market

What is the over the counter market? The over the counter market, known as the OTCBB, which stands for Over The Counter Market Bulletin Board, is a regulated quotation service that displays real time quotes, last sale prices, and volume information in over the counter equity securities. An OTC security is any stock that does not trade on Nasdaq or a national securities exchange. OTCBB stocks include national, regional, and foreign equity issues, warrants, units, American Depositary Receipts and Direct Participation Programs.

The OTC market was started in June 1990 on a trial basis as part of a wide range of market reforms that were taking place at the time. The aim of the market reforms was to make the OTC equity markets more transparent. The Penny Stock Reform Act of 1990 mandated the U.S. Securities and Exchange Commission to institute an electronic system that would abide by the rules of Section 17B of the Exchange Act. The purpose of the new electronic system was to enable the spread and circulation of price quotes and trade transactions. Starting December 1993 firms have been required to report trades in all domestic OTC equity series through the Automated Confirmation Transaction Service (ACT) within 90 seconds of the transaction. This system enables anyone form the largest firm to the smallest investor to know how many trades are taking place in a stock, the direction of the trades, buys or sells, and the volume in real time.

In April 1997 the Securities and Exchange Commission approved the operation of the OTCBB on a permanent basis with

some modifications. Even up to that point OTC quoted companies were not responsible to file quarterly and yearly financial reports. Due to the lack of the reporting requirement it became
increasingly difficult to research a company. Many companies
traded without having to file any financial information. N investor
would have to rely on press releases and communication with the
company for all information. It became very difficult to verify a
press release since the releases were vague and left allot to the imagination. A company could issue a release saying that they grossed
$15 million dollars in the third quarter. Now that number sounds
exciting but we do not know what their expenses were for the
quarter. We also do not know the size of the company's debt, or
even when the debt needs to be paid off. Many investors would see
the release and jump to conclusions only to find that the company
sent out another release later on announcing that they had a severe
cash flow problem and were looking for to raise funds. The flip
side also took place where many investors stayed away from what
could have been a lifetime opportunity due to the lack of information. Many companies issued positive releases but were ignored by
investors who could not find the financials they were looking for.
Keep in mind that many companies today that trade for over $50
once traded for under a $1, including Microsoft, MCI, Toys R Us,
and many others.

　　To alleviate this issue the Securities and Exchange Commission approved the OTCBB Eligibility Rule. The Eligibility Rule
dictated that all non-reporting OTC companies already trading
on the OTC market would have to report their financial information to the SEC, banking, or insurance regulators in order to meet
eligibility requirements. A phase in period was set for all trading
companies starting in alphabetical order from the beginning of
July 1999 to June 2000. As the phase in date for a company passed
if the company had still not reported its financials the ticker symbol would receive an extra e added. A symbol would now carry an
extra e at the end letting investors know that the company had not
reported its financials. The non-reporting company was then given

30 days to report. If the company did not report in that 30 day grace period the stock was delisted from the OTC and moved to the pink sheets. (We will discuss the pink sheets in the next chapter.) The benefit of this rule is that as of now any stock traded on the OTC market has publicly available financials. The financials can be accessed through Edgar or through other financial databases. The benefit of this is that in the past a company might have been able to work in the shadows without limited oversight. The company could put out ambiguous press releases with little concern over the accuracy of the announcements. Now that every OTC company needs to file financials with the SEC they are forced to hire accountants and lawyers who are familiar with all the requirements. The management of the public company will go out of its way to make sure that its financial statements are accurate and precise. The SEC would not hesitate to suspend trading in a stock that it suspected of fraud. A suspension would be the smallest of their problems since the SEC would not let any a company off the hook if it participated in fraud. The bureaucrats in Washington realize that the reason so many international and domestic investors participate in our public markets is because of the high level of trust they have over the efficient and honest structure of our markets. Every time a company is engaged in fraud the luster of our markets faces the risk of being diminished. The SEC knows this and is therefore very strict when it comes to reviewing and accepting financials.

The strict requirements imposed on public companies are quite advantageous for the average investor. Instead of having to guess the condition of a financial company all the investor needs to do is call the company and request their latest financials. The company then has the obligation to open up its books and ensure that the investor has access to its most current filings. And now that the deadline has passed for all public companies to be fully reporting the investor can be rest assured that any OTC traded company is filling. The first step in analyzing a company is to take a step inside and pretend that you are its auditor. By printing out a copy of the company's financials you will now know just as much about them as their own auditor. That is as long as you learn how to read the financials.

The following are some basic statistics concerning the OTC market. The OTC Bulletin Board market provides access to over 6500 different companies. It is estimated that one third of them will remain on the OTC market after meeting the eligibility requirements. As is often the case, many of the companies that do not meet the requirements and are moved to the pink sheets will file at a later point in an attempt to move back to the OTC. The OTC market consists of more than 400 Market Makers.

The Market Makers are the dealers who compete to buy and sell your shares. They set their own bid and asks for the stocks traded on the market. A typical market maker will set his bid at .24 and his ask at .26. He will buy shares from investors at .25 and sell them at .26. Now you might wonder what would prevent an MM from setting his bid way below the ask so he can derive a greater profit from the spread. Many Market Makers do try to widen the bid and ask as much as they can since they are looking to profit from the difference between the bid and the ask, what we call the spread. While a Market Maker chooses how he wants to set the spread he will have competitive pressures. If one MM decides to keep his spread at .02, another market maker might jump in an decide that he is willing to keep his spread at only a cent. The brokers will route their orders to the Market Maker with the best price. So the second MM will now receive the order flow from the brokers. Now the second market maker has set his bid at .25 and his ask at .26 it means that investors selling their stock to this market maker will receive one cent more then if they had sold to previous MM. Now what often occurs is that one market maker might be more interested in buying than in selling. He will raise his bid but keep the ask the same. You will see the bid raised to .255 and the ask will remain at .26. Or another market maker might enter the fray and realizing how much of a demand there is for the stock he will raise his bid to .27 hoping to buy up all the shares available. Why would he do this? He might be convinced that the stock will soon be trading at .30 due to the high demand building up. He will then raise his bid to .27 and his ask to .28 so he can sell his shares for a profit. Now the other Market Makers have a choice, they can either hope that the other Market Maker stops buying shares and lowers his bid and ask or they can match his price. If they do not match his price then all the buys and sells will be directed to the new MM who is offering the best price. Like in the real world, all the sellers will now sell to him since he is willing to pay the most. Now the other MMs will watch the activity very closely. If they sense that the availability of shares is drying up they will be forced to move up their bid so they can also buy stocks to resell later on. Very often this happens so fast that the market makers are caught off guard and do not have any shares to sell to the public. They will have to rapidly increase their bids so they can buy shares. They are most likely selling shares they do not have in their hands in the hope that they will be able to buy them later. But until they can find sellers from whom to buy the shares they will have to keep increasing their bid. They also raise their asks in tandem with the bids so they can sell the shares they are buying to the ravenous buyers. When the amount of shares (the supply) is smaller than the number of buy orders (the demand) the price rapidly increases. Most OTC stocks trade for under a dollar and never experience any large publicity. But once they do experience a moment in the spotlight you will see many, sometimes thousands of investors, rushing to buy the stock. But since the float of the stock might only consist of 1,000,000 shares there will not be nearly enough shares for all of the buyers. The market makers will want to buy and sell the stock since they make their money in stocks experiencing large amounts of volume. They will set bid and asks for the stock hoping to be able to buy and sell the volatile stocks. But the only way for them to keep up with dramatic surge in volume will be to raise their prices as much as they need to in order to buy stocks from the public. They will also raise the price they are willing to sell their shares to the buyers when they determine how much the buyers are willing to pay for them. I have seen many stocks issue positive news and then have the price of their stocks double the same day. The floats were often small and the investors felt that the stock was worth many more times than what they paid for it. I have also seen stocks like EPWN move from .09 to $8 in four months on a steady release of positive news. The market makers make money regardless of the price of the stock since they will always sell it for less than they buy it and buy it for less than they sell it.

The difference between the OTCBB market and the Nasdaq is that OTC companies do not have listing standards. The Nasdaq has very strict qualifications for letting a company list its stock on its exchange. The OTC allows any company that files its statements to trade on its market. The Nasdaq requires a company to meet asset and revenue criteria while an OTC company does not need to have any assets or revenues. Many Nasdaq companies that fall into financial harships are often removed from the Nasdaq due to their inability to meet listing requirements. They might have either lost a large percentage of their assets or revenues and are most likely in bankruptcy proceedings. Once their share price falls and stays below a certain price thresh hold for an extended period they are removed from the Nasdaq and then resume trading on the OTC market. The most important difference between them is probably that the OTC market does not provide automated trade executions. It is up to the Market Maker to decide if he wants to buy your stock. He can sit and wait and watch the direction of the market or he can simply decide not to buy it. Chances are that if a Market Maker does not act on an order the brokerage house will stop sending trades in his direction. Once a Market Maker develops a reputation for not acting on orders in timely fashion the brokerage houses will choose not deal with him. What a Market Maker will do when he does not want to act on the order is that he will change his price. If he does not want to buy your BICO for .22 he will lower his bid for .21. This way he does not appear to be ignoring the order. He is also hoping that you will lower your price until he decides to buy it. He can keep lowering his bid until he decides that the stock is now cheap enough for him. After buying your shares he will raise the bid if he has to buy more shares from other investors. The MM will not do this if there is allot of volume since in that situation he would just want to be able to quickly buy and sell your shares. But the above does happen when you are dealing with a stock with minimal volume. If you are the only sell that day and there have been no buys the MM will not be in a rush to buy your shares since he will most likely be stock with the shares for a while.

CHAPTER 3

The Pink Sheets

There is another corner of the securities market where one can find exciting opportunities if she does her proper diligence and research. This small market resembles the era of the wild west. There are almost no rules and hardly any oversight. Companies in this dark corner of the financial world are not required to file financial statements and do not even have to issue an annual report. Most of these companies do not ever plan on moving to the OTC and many of them do not even have ongoing operations. Now before you are lead to think that this market consists of a handful of mom and pop stores masquerading as public companies hold on. This market is actually home to over 20,000 stocks. For many reasons they have chosen to remain on the pink sheets. They might have decided that they do not want to have to open up their books for all their competitors to see. Once they file their financials they can expect a total loss of privacy since the SEC wants to know exactly how each executive is being compensated and what the assets the company owns. The SEC will demand that the company states exactly to whom and how much it owes. Many smaller companies do not want to have to give out all this privileged information at this period of their business. If they are embarking on a new business venture they might opt to keep all of their information a secret. But due to the lack of information available on stocks trading on the pink sheets a large majority of investors stay away from them. To make matters even worse the Market Makers who set markets in pink sheet stocks keep a very large spread. It is very common for a stock in the pink sheets to have a bid of .05 and an ask of .25.

Why do they keep such a large spread? The Market Maker might feel that the stock has no buyers and sellers for it. He does not want to buy the stock only to be stuck with it for a year until another buyer comes along. By keeping the spread wide he discourages investors from wanting to buy the stock. At .05 the bid is only a fifth of the ask. The bid would have go up 500% before it even equaled the ask. The dual purpose of this large spread is that if an investor does decide to buy or sell the stock the MM has locked in a tremendous profit for later on in the event that the stock does experience large activity.

Many pink sheet stocks do have spreads of less than a penny so it pays for an investor to take the pink sheets very seriously. Most pink sheet stocks have been beaten down so far in price that they often trade at less than their book value. A company with a book value of $1,000,000 may only have a market cap of $20,000. The number of authorized shares could be 20,000,000 and the stock could trade at .01 a share. But what makes this stock even more potentially profitable is that the float, or the number of available shares in the market, might be allot smaller. The float for the above company might only be 2,000,000. That would mean that the total price for all of the shares in the market is only $20,000 giving the stock a market cap of only $20,000. That means that you would be able to buy all the available shares of a public company with a book value of a $1,000,000 for only $20,000. If this company went on to become a reporting company it would attract allot of more attention. Investors would then start realizing how undervalued the company is. Then if the company followed through and augmented its current line of business and increased its profits you could be sure that allot of penny stock investors would start trying to buy the stock. But guess what? You own all of the shares of the company. The Market Makers would raise their bids hoping to get you to sell your shares so they can sell them to the new buyers. It would then be up to you to decide if you felt that the price could go allot higher if you are satisfied enough with your current profit. Now lets be more realistic, not everyone would put down $20,000 on a stock that might never pick up and is highly illiquid. Assuming that you spent a month researching this company and decided that this company really had something going for it. You might have discovered a patent they hold is worth a great deal once it is developed. Or maybe they own the rights to a clothing line with a vast consumer base in Texas and the CEO has finally decided to give it a try and enter the Texas market. So you buy a quarter of the available shares for $5,000 and wait to see how they fear in their new business. Now lets compute what your shares would be worth now if they become successful. The CEO decides that it is time to garner recognition and money from the investor community so he hires a CPA who files all the necessary financials to become an OTC traded security. The company becomes reporting and the stock moves from .01 to .05 based on its low valuation compared to other fully reporting OTC stocks. The company then announces that they are opening a new sales outlet in San Antonio Texas. The sales outlet is expected to generate $50,000 in earnings. Now remember that the reason you were able to buy the stock for so low was probably because the company had no earnings at the time and probably was doing minimal business if any. Now that the company is forecasting earnings investors will try to approximate a price earnings ratio and buy the stock based on the PE. Assuming that the company will earn a net profit of $50,000 we will now divide that amount by the number of shares in the float. There are 2 million shares in the float so if the company earns a $50,000 profit each stock will actually represent .025 of profit per share. With the stock trading at .05 the stock is only trading at two times its earnings, or a PE of 2. Now investors will start noticing the stock and say that most clothing retailers trade in PE multiples of 15 so this stock will be worth .375 if the company does earn $50,000. Now that those investors have noticed how undervalued it is compared to other clothing retailers they will start buying up the stock until it is close to what they feel is the price it should be trading at. Assuming that after a few weeks of buying the stock settles at .35 a share you have made a decent profit. This price is still under what most investors have valued the stock at. Now what would happen if the company earned $500,000 instead of $50,000? Logic would stipulate that the stock would now be worth 10 times as much, or $3.75. Looking back at the beginning of this equation you will see that you purchased 500,000 shares for $5,000. With the stock trading at .35 your stake is worth now $175,000. Not bad for an original investment of $5,000.

How do you find the right penny stock? It is much more challenging to find a profitable penny stock due to the lack of transparency. There are no public financials to read. There is no current annual report to compare to the previous year's annual report. So how would you begin? Your first step is to select an industry that you understand. We all have a hobby or a line of work we can talk about for hours. If you have not been able to tell yet, my line of work is penny stock investing. I can tell you war stories for hours and on about hundreds of situations I have seen develop in the micro cap world. If you have a line of work that you are intimately familiar with you will want to use it as a starting point for your pink sheet stock research. Employees in the banking industry might want to research banks trading on the pink sheets. Another approach is to investigate companies dealing in your favorite hobby. Movie fans might want to research film production companies trading on the pink sheets. A movie fan might know which movies have potential and might have a feel for upcoming talent. If the movie buff feels that the combination of a great cast and plot of an upcoming movie will take Hollywood by storm he might decide to buy stock in that company. If the movie is successful then the production company should enjoy some nice profits.

The next step in researching penny stocks is more time consuming but is where the real challenge starts. Imagine you are the movie buff mentioned above. You really like the idea of a movie mixing political intrigue and dramatic war footage in the deserts of Africa. You can picture yourself seeing the movie a few times. You have read the resumes and seen the pictures of the cast. You are impressed on how the production company was able to get a list of popular actors to star in their upcoming film. You know what it takes for a movie to receive great reviews and you are sure that this movie will receive the best reviews when it is nationally released. Sounds like you have found the perfect penny stock company. They have a great product with a large market. The movie industry is highly profitable and there are many companies making money in it. Before you pick up the phone and call your broker you still need to take a few more steps.

The next day you will want to go to your local library and pick up a few trade publications covering the film industry. Read the articles and familiarize yourself with the business aspect of the movie business. You want to decide if the movie industry as a whole is growing or if it is in decline. If you read that the movie business is expected to grow by 25% for the next three years you know you are on to something. If the next article states that there is a lack of production companies in the filed then you know that there is a market for the company's service. You want to make an educated guess based on your reading if there is room for another production company or if the field is crowded. You will want to walk out of the library with a firm grasp of the industry. If it takes you 4 or 5 visits to the library it is worth each and every visit.

Your third day investigating this company should be spent first by compiling a list of pertinent questions for the company. Spend time developing educated questions based on your readings on the industry. Make sure that your questions are direct and to the point. If you are put through to the CEO he will not have much time to spend talking to you so you want to make the most of the time available. If your questions show him that you have researched the industry and are genuinely interested in his company he will enjoy talking to you. In the event that he is busy request a time when you can call him. He will most likely give you a time the next day when he has a few minutes available. Make sure to develop a relationship with him or her so you can call them from time to time to receive updates on the company. A clear warning sign would be a company that did not want to speak to you. If a company has no interest in speaking to investors it is most likely due to their lack of activity then anything else. Dormant companies have nothing to. Many times stock promoters will buy up shares in a dormant company, issue a few press releases and then dump the stock on to unsuspecting investors. Research and communication is the key. The more you know about the company the more you will be able to determine if they are for real and what their prospects are.

The information you need the most from the CEO or their investor relations spokesperson are, the number of authorized and outstanding shares, financial condition of the company, insider ownership, institutional ownership, and upcoming business developments. Keep in mind that they will only volunteer this information once you establish a rapport with them and show them that you are serious about becoming a long term investor. Many companies do move from the pink sheets to the OTC and some even to the Nasdaq, so if you do your research correctly you should be able to find some hidden gems.

CHAPTER 4

Research Tools

There are many research tools available to the investor. Just like there are many different types of investors there are also many different types of research tools. Bloomberg is a financial information provider that provides up to the minute news and filings on public companies along with business news and analytical articles on companies and events. There are many articles that cover the possible impact of an international event on the financial markets. Investors need to know what the acceptance of China as a trading partner means to the price of Hong Kong stocks. Investors rely on the up to the minute news on prices and events in real time. Due to its high cost Bloomberg has been restricted to professional traders and brokers. There are other free tools such as FinanceYahoo.com a web site dedicated to providing delayed quotes along with press releases and filings from public companies. The following chapter will provide you with an ample amount of research tools along with a brief explanation on them along with information on how to use them to research OTC stocks.

Silicon Investor.com

The Silicon Investor web site is one of the most well known web sites catering to active traders. The site provides news, analyzes, and message boards. You can obtain real time quotes on the home page. A portfolio tool is available in which you can enter the stocks you have bought along with the prices you paid for the stocks.

The portfolio will keep track of your investment's performance based on the price and date you input. Financial news is updated on an hourly basis. There is a section entitled Hot Stock Talk listing the top 10 most active threads on the site. Market Insight provides ongoing articles written by the web site's columnists.

Distinguishing this site from many other financial sites is the plethora of message boards offered. There are message boards on every conceivable stock and investment topic. You can start a message board on a given topic if you do not find one suiting your interest. There are message boards where you can read postings on stock picks from other investors. You will find message boards discussing a dollar and under stocks. In the dollar and under message board a poster will discuss a stock trading for under a dollar. What most often occurs is that an investor will first read about a stock in a newsletter. The investor will turn the site and post the name of the stock along with a request for information from other investors who might be familiar with it. Sometimes within minutes of his posting investors will reply with information on the company. The posters will share past experiences they have had with the stock. Information will start pouring out concerning the company before the investors resume posting messages on their previously discussed topic. You can also look for a message board on a particular stock where you will most likely find investors who expect the stock to do well and other investors who are convinced the company is heading for bankruptcy.

Another great facet of this site is its access to research tools. There is a stock screener that can be used to search for stocks that meet your criteria. You can obtain a list of stocks with a market cap of under $5,000,000 or request a list of stocks with growing earnings. You can combine various criteria to produce a narrow list of companies meeting your investment strategy. If you want companies trading for under $1 a share with growing earnings of 20% or more, and market caps of under $5,000,000 you would only need to select that information in the stock screener and let the screener produce a list of a handful of companies. You would then take that list of companies and research the stocks using other web sites and research techniques that will be discussed in this book. Silicon Investor University is a resource of educational material for the growing investor. There are courses on Investing, Business and Management, Entrepreneurial Skills, and Personal Finance. You can also find a Market Tool menu in the site. The section has a Market Monitor, Up/Downgrades, Movers and Shakers, Bond Market Snap Shot, IPOs and Reuters Top News. Market Monitor delivers a quick snapshot of key indices and indicators. Up/Downgrades provides recent changes to key analyst opinions. Movers and Shakers shows you what is hot and what is cold. Bond Market Snap Shot offers key bond pricing and yield curve. IPOs updates you on recent filings, pricings and after-market reports. Reuters Top News informs you with the latest financial and political news.

Annual reports on 4,000 companies are available for free. The Calendar section of the site keeps track of upcoming stock splits, expected earnings, economic events, and reported earnings along with positive and negative surprises. Membership in the site costs $120 annually.

Dimgroup.com

Dimgroup.com is an interesting site for investors who are new to the mechanisms of the penny stock market. The site is divided in seven sections. OTC Central, Premier Articles, Nasdaq, Stock Tools, Stock Humor, This Week, and Trader News. OTC Central is highly recommended since it supplies a complete directory of OTC stocks. Along with a complete listing you will be able to use the section to find profiles consisting of financials, filings, and charts for many OTC stocks. Rankings are given for many OTC stocks using industry and overall rankings. In the section you will have access to 10sb filings, rules and reports. A link to the web site's 2500 message boards will give you immediate exposure to what investors are saying regarding a particular stock you are investigating.

Premier Articles is a unique section. There are many sites supplying articles concerning penny stock practices. You can go to almost any site and read about how a market maker operates, remember, the market maker is the middleman who buys and sells the stocks that investors trade. The way this section differentiates itself from other sites that provide similar information is by using message boards. Next to each article there is a message board discussing the article. For example, as of the writing of the book, there is an article entitled "Ways of a Market Maker". Next to the article you can read messages posted by investors reminiscing over experiences that the article describes. Investors explain how they used the information from the article to beat the market maker at its own game. If the article says that market makers tend to sell their holdings at the end of the month and buy them at the beginning of the month, you would know that stocks will generally move down the last few days of the month and recover the first few days of the next month. You might even read a message by a poster who writes how a certain market maker is known for playing with the price of the stock and with investors' pocket books. You would be well advised to watch out when that market maker is the one acting as a middleman for the stock you are considering trading.

Nasdaq provides information on short positions, upcoming IPOs, and technical analysis.

Two stock tool programs on the site help calculate your profits and determine what your average cost for a stock is. Average cost is the cost of a stock bought at different prices. If you purchased 100,000 shares of ARET at .05 and 200,000 shares at .08 your average cost would be .07 a share. You can calculate this by multiplying the number of shares you bought by the price you paid for them and then doing the same for the other purchase of the stock. You then divide the total purchase cost by the number of shares and you will have the average price that you paid for each share. Repeat the next steps on a piece of paper and see if you understand the formula. A) 100,000 x .05 = $5,000 B) 200,000 x .08 = $16,000 C) $5,000 + $16,000 = $21,000 D) 21,000 / 300,000

= .07 We divided the money spent buying the shares by the total
number of shares owned, resulting in an average price of .07 per
share.

Every investor needs to take time off from the serious pursuit
of investing. It is easy to spend hours doing diligent research. By
the time you are ready to leave your computer you have looked at
countless spreadsheets and read hundreds of press releases. The
last thing you want to do is look at anything related to investing
for the next 17 hours until the market resumes business. But what
if you are starting to feel your head becoming cloudy with the
constant computation of facts and numbers? The answer is the
Stock Humor page. The Stock Humor Page pokes fun at many
investor strategies and contemporary issues. You would be surprised what you can learn from humor at the same time as you
laugh your head off at some of the sarcastic articles with names like
PumpDump.com and The Well Street Journal.

This Week notifies readers to the companies releasing earnings
that week and provides a list of IPOs scheduled for the current
week. If any statistics are being released in the next few days this
section is the best place to check.

The last section in the web site but arguably the most important is Trader News. The section provides important news that
deals with subjects pertaining to all serious and sophisticated investors. You will find articles titled "SEC Halts Fraudulent Securities" describing a recent move by the SEC to halt securities deemed
to be fraudulent. After reading this article you should become
aware to some of the perils of investing in small companies. The
benefit of reading an article like the above mentioned is that you
should be able to use the supplied information in the article to
recognize stocks that might be suspended by the SEC in the future. If you read in the article that the SEC suspended trading in
a company after receiving complaints from investors that no one
ever answered the phone at the corporate offices, you should be
wary of any companies that do not answer their phones. Of course,
the reasons for suspending trading in a stock are always more complex

but share certain basic similarities. The key is to study companies that have had their shares suspended. You need to learn everything about them so you can recognize the warning signs in other stocks before they are suspended. The only worse thing than investing in a fraudulent security is holding it when it gets suspended. Once you learn how to differentiate the losers from the winners you will be half way to becoming wealthy through investing.

PCQuote.com

This site has it all. From multiple quotes, to symbol lookups, charts, options, futures, research, breaking news provided by CNNfn.com, a trading bookshop, trading software, and a section with mini courses. The site lists quotes for the 10 top requested quotes. The list is a good idea if you want to get a good feeling to which stocks are the most actively followed. If you see that a stock is on the list chances is that there are many short-term trades involved with the stock.

OTC Investor

OTC Investor is a free investment resource that provides individual investors with small and micro-cap companies before those companies receive recognition from Wall Street. The featured companies often trade on the Over the Counter Bulletin Board Exchange. The web site profiles companies involved in high tech industries such as the Internet, Electronics, Bio Technology, and Computing. The site feels that the companies it features are poised for rapid stock price growth due to a number of factors including upcoming products, new partners, strategic alliances, financing, and upcoming news announcements. The site offers a free newsletter covering the stocks they feature.

Subscriptions are available on the site for the following newsletters: BFN Updates, Ahead of Street, Stockconference.com, Hi-Tech Hangout, OTC Stock Picks, Small Cap Forum, and the SciTech Investor.

StockMaster.com

You will find a list of the day's most active stocks broken down by most active, big gainers, and big losers. Redherring.com provides news. The site has appeals to investors who need cut and dry information on companies without the fluff found on many sites.

Stock-Rave

Stock-Rave promotes itself as the site where you can find the resources to make wiser investment decisions in the penny stock market. They have guides regarding the rules and regulations of trading pennies, and what to watch out for. There are even a couple of mailing lists for the members and guests of the site to choose from, one of which is The Penny Stock News Play List, which sends out news alerts that should have a favorable impact on a particular stock. There is also a comprehensive links section that will direct you to various investment articles, tools, resources, and other penny stock related sites. The site has a Penny Pick of the Week Contest in which the stock pick that performs the largest gain over a week's period is declared the winner.

Micro Cap World.com

Micro Cap World describes itself as the information source for qualified OTC Bulletin Board stocks. They have strict eligibility requirements that a stock must meet before it can be featured on the site. Only OTC stocks that have been recommended by a Broker/Dealer or "Non-Compensated" financial publication will be featured on the site. The site provides additional information the featured companies including news, charts, quotes, and links.

Fairshare

Interesting site where you can learn about Venture Capital and be exposed to opportunities for small investors.

Future Super Stock.com

Provides profiles on small to medium sized growth companies that are publicly traded. Free services include Hot Breaking News, Company Profiles, and Stock Quotes. The site receives compensation by the companies that it covers. You should do your own research and only use this site to get ideas. Since they are receiving compensation by the featured companies the site will feature all types of companies. You need to keep in mind that they will make sure to point out the positive aspects, while sometimes ignoring the perils the company faces.

Raging Bull.com

Raging Bull is my favorite site on the Internet when it comes to investing. The site is an incredible assortment of useful information. The home page features a Top Stories section. Top Stories is usually two stories that are updated on a daily basis. The two stories deal with the market as a whole and with particular companies. If a large merger has just been announced you will find a story on it in this section. You can read what the effect of the merger will be on similar companies in the same field and to the market as whole. For example, if IBM and Apple decided to merge, you would find an article on the merger detailing the effect of the combination of these two giants on the many other smaller computers companies. I can assure you that if this merger ever took place you see a steady drop in price in small computer stocks. The reason for the drop in price in the smaller computer stocks is that smaller computer companies would find it harder to compete with the new giant in the field. The flip side would be reading that a large company is now leaving the market making room for the small computer companies. Then the price of their stocks would surly rise in price.

What Raging Bull is most known for is its message boards. Active traders make sure to read the message boards on an hourly basis to see if investors are bullish or bearish on a stock they own. This is crucial with smaller stocks where investors can change their perception on a stock within minutes of a press release. If a press release is issued by ABC Incorporated saying that they are closing their factory in China, you would be well advised to read the message board for that stock to see how investors feel about the news. If they feel that the news is negative for the prospects of the company the price of the stock could lose 40% of its value within an hour. On the other hand, if investors are glad that the company will spend its money elsewhere the price of the stock could advance by 50% before the day is over.

The day's top posts are collected in the Herd on the Boards section. Go to this section to see what sophisticated investors are discussing. The selected posts are the one most often read by other investors. Keep in mind that many posters, people who post messages on the boards, have large followings. There are investors who have been posting messages on the boards for years and have a large following from investors who have benefited from their predictions.

Raging News and Editorial is a section comprised of Raging Bull writers covering investment topics pertaining to the general market, business, analysts, and Internet investing. The topics change on a daily basis.

Today's Most Active Message Boards is a unique concept among all message board sites. Raging Bull keeps track of the most active message boards and lists the top 10 on the site. The list is determined by measuring the relative number of posts per board over the last 8 hours. The list is updated hourly. This is great if you want to know what the most active talked about stocks are in any given hour. You can benefit two ways from this. You can either look for stocks that have many investors discussing the stock knowing that there are many investors considering buying or selling the stock. If they are getting ready to buy the stock you can be sure that the price will rise accordingly. The other way to benefit from this feature is by learning from the discussions. If you notice that the top most active board covers a gambling stock you can be sure that there is an event looming that will have a drastic effect on the price. In this case, the Senate was debating a gambling bill in which they were considering making online gambling illegal. If the bill passed many penny stocks that conducted online gambling operations would be driven out of business. By reading the most active message boards you will find out about events affecting not only the penny stock discussed but other penny stocks in the same business segment.

My favorite aspect of this wonderful site is the plethora of message boards. You can find boards on any stock in the market. If you cannot find a board discussing your stock you can simply send an email to the staff at Raging Bull and they will start the board for you. You post messages by using a screen name you obtain upon registering at the site. Registration is free at the site. We will learn in a later chapter how to effectively maximize your investing by using the message boards for research purposes.

Bloomberg.com

Bloomberg is known as the most comprehensive source of financial and business news. The Bloomberg network consists of a television station, a radio station, and a web site. Bloomberg also publishes books and magazines, and the online Bloomberg institute, providing free online courses.

The Bloomberg web site provides quotes, news, and proprietary articles. Every major index is reported and updated on a regular basis. There is a section on the site labeled the Entrepreneur Network. The Network contains a feature story about an entrepreneur who has an inspirational story where he or she overcame a major obstacle and beat the odds against success. You will also find products and services that are helpful in starting a small business along with a tip of the week.

Now you must be asking yourself how this information powerhouse can help you invest in penny stocks. The answer is that the site will update you on all trends that are developing in the market. Penny stocks are heavily influenced by the general trends of the market. During the height of the Internet euphoria many penny stocks doubled and tripled in very short periods. Often penny stock companies that announced the launching of an e-commerce site experienced a 100% price gain within the week. Yes, you read it correctly; you could have seen an investment of $5,000 grow to $10,000 before the week was up.

Right now the DNA research sector seems to be heating up. With all the promises that a human blueprint map holds there are many investors starting to focus on the field. Many large and small companies that specialize in DNA research have already seen their stocks appreciate over 40%. One small stock that I bought last week, CLYC, more than doubled from .04 to .09 in one week after announcing a reverse merger with a private DNA research firm. How could you have predicted that the DNA filed would start heating up? You could have started reading the articles that Bloomberg was carrying on this field. I think this field has much more potential than people have realized. Scientists at CLYC are predicting that they will soon know which genes cause allergic reactions to prescribed drugs. If they are able to accomplish this they will be able to warn patients not to take medicine that will cause them unsuspected adverse reactions. This field will prove to be very controversial since we will soon know which genes are prone to cause certain diseases. Once an insurance company knows that an individual carries the genes that lead to cancer will they want to insure him? Will rates be lowered if an individual can show his insurer that his genes insulate him from most diseases? You can be certain that there will be billions of dollars invested in DNA research in the coming years.

Most stock quotations provided only let you look quotes for listed and OTC securities. It is very rare to find a site providing quotes for pink sheet stocks. Once you do find a site with access to pink sheet stocks you will not have the bid and ask price for them, you will only have the price of the last trade. Here is the other benefit of using the Bloomberg web site. When you enter a quote for a pink sheet stock you will see the bid and ask, last trade, high and low for the day, and the total volume. Information is the lifeblood of this business. Without as much information as you can find you are flying blind. You would not want to place an order for a pink sheet stock that is starting to get sold off. A great pink sheet stock that is getting sold off will fall much faster than an OTC stock due to liquidity problems. The market maker will not buy as many shares since he is unsure if he will have a buyer later for them. So as the sell orders pour in he will keep lowering the price he is willing to buy them for. That is why looking at the last trade is so important. If you are thinking of placing an order for any stock, especially a pink sheet stock, you want to see if the last 10 trades were buys or sells. If they were sells it means people are exiting their positions and the price will decline. If they are buys people are accumulating to their positions and taking new positions in the stock. Bloomberg will provide the last trade for the stock and let you know if it was a buy or sell. If you are using another quotation system and want to know if a trade was a buy or sell look at the current bid and ask. If the trade was at the bid it was a sell and a buy if it was at the ask.

OTCNews.com

This site is a source for OTC Company news, live OTCBB stock quotes, press release service for companies, and OTC BB Company Web Site Hosting.

Penny Stock Insider.com

This is an interesting site for penny stock investors. I am fond of the free customized reports. You can obtain free reports pertaining to penny stocks. Recently, the following reports were available.

Free Hot List Stock Picks, Free List of Penny Stocks, Feature Articles, and How To Evaluate Those Stock Tips You Hear From Friends and Co-Workers.

Look at the section for new investors. This section alone should be able to provide enough information to make the novice feel like he has been around the block once or twice. Even after reading this book you might find that you still have some questions. Later on you might across a term you are unfamiliar with. The New Investors area provides introductions to investing and penny stocks. There are answers to frequently asked questions, a glossary of stock market terms, and more.

Penny Stock Research Center is the center for powerful research tips and tools for penny stocks. You need to become a member to obtain full access to the site.

OTCBB.Com

This is the official site for the OTC Bulletin Board. You will find all pertinent information on the OTC Bulletin Board market along with information on the securities traded. OTCBB.com offers Market Statistics and Trading Activity Reports, which give you a general oversight of the market. Total share and dollar volume for the market are important gauges of the liquidity of the market. Using the two above-mentioned selections you can keep track of the direction of the OTC market. If you see volume drying up compared to the last quarter then you know that there is not as much money in the market as there was in the past. The lack of money will prevent stocks from rising as much as they could in a better market. A lower dollar volume will also mean that the transactions are much smaller. If instead of investors buying and selling $10 million worth of securities on a given day, they are now only trading a fraction of that amount, you will find it harder to move in and out of a position. This is because people are buying and selling a smaller amount of stocks than they were previously. Try to unload a million shares of a stock when the average trade is only for 1000 shares and you will see the price plummet since there are no buyers for a million shares. The same would happen if you try to buy 100,000 shares of a stock that has not traded in a few weeks. The market maker will raise the price since his supply is low and he needs to encourage investors to sell him the stock so he can fulfill your order. You want to keep abreast of the health of the general OTC market to determine the best periods to place your trades. In an illiquid market with low volume you are better off not selling since the price will be more susceptible to sells. You would wait for a high volume period before placing a large buy so your trade would not stand out and force the market maker to raise the price.

The OTCBB provides contact information for all reporting issues that trade on its market along with contact information for the market makers who buy and sell the securities. General news is provided in conjunction with a information on stocks that have been halted. The SEC may halt stocks that it suspects of fraud or of trading irregularities. Recommended reading for ambitious penny stock investors is the OTCBB News area. There are many changes that both the SEC and the OTC institute to create a more efficient market. This year an eligibility requirement was implemented for all stocks quoted on the over the counter market. OTC stocks needed to file their financials with the SEC by a phase in date. The SEC would review the financials and send them back to the company with comments. Once the company answered all comments it would have its financials cleared by the Security Exchange Commission. The stock of the company would continue trading on the over the counter market. If a company missed the date or did not submit financials it would receive an E added to its ticker symbol as a warning that the stock would be de listed within 30 days if it did not file its financials. Stocks that did not submit and have their financials approved by the SEC were de listed to the pink sheets. During this time much confusion arose over the dates that stocks had until to get their financials approved. Many investors did not understand what the extra E meant. Some investors bought the stocks that were about to become de listed after their prices dropped. What those investors did not realize was that the reason the prices were dropping was because investors were bailing out of stocks that would soon trade on the pink sheets. All of the problems that arose from the confusion could have been remedied by reading all about the eligibility rule. Everything there was to know about the rule was on the OTCBB web site along with a calendar and dates for each stock. By checking the date when your stock would need to report by you could take an educated guess if you felt that the company had enough time to file its financials. Many companies missed the cut off dates but later re listed on the OTC after having their financials approved.

More recently, the SEC implemented an OTCBB trade halt authority. The SEC can now halt trading for two weeks in a company's stock when the company has issued a false press release. An example of this would be when a company recently bought a product from a major telecommunications firm and claimed that they had become a strategic partner to the telecommunications giant. The SEC halted trading in the stock until the small company issued a retraction explaining the actual relationship it had with the larger company. Upon resuming of trading the stock lost 50% of its value. Lesson for investors, make sure to check out all press releases or you will learn the hard way that what seems too good to be true usually is. Read the OTCBB News section daily to read about regulatory changes that can affect your trading strategies.

OTC Digest.com

OTC Digest is one of the leading online sources of information in the financial newsletter industry. The authors of the digest feel that the featured companies are the undiscovered gems of the small cap market. The editorial staff brings updated and unbiased information on a weekly basis. OTC Digest follows low priced Nasdaq and OTC Bulletin Board opportunities that they feel are fundamentally undervalued and under-followed.

The Digest profiles relatively low-cap stocks and continually seeks out high growth companies that command strength and the ability to impact the market place with innovative products and services. Each issue of OTC Digest gives a weekly update on each stock and its listings, and highlights a company from time to time, with a special Situation Report for discussion. OTC Digest's editors meet with the directors of each company to discuss in detail their fundamentals and when possible, visit the Corporate Headquarters. OTC Digest also keeps its readers abreast of general developments in each related field of research and product development, and reports in depth on each company's progress. You need to subscribe to receive via email a complimentary subscription to the OTC Digest.

OTCFN.com

The OTC Financial Network rates itself as the premier financial communications and investor relations firm for small/ micro cap public companies. Companies pay them for their public relations service. On the site you will find a list of their clients and the latest press releases for their clients.

Stock Guide.com

Stock Guide provides convenience and access in one place. You can use their site to find quotes, charts, and SEC filings of a company. On the opening page you can type in the ticker symbol of the company and see all the SEC documents that the company has filed. This is an easy and fast way to find out if the company has recently increased the number of shares outstanding or undertaken any major changes in the corporate structure. This retrieval tool will also pull up all the quarterly reports and annual reports for the company. A list of all OTC companies is enclosed in the site. Custom reports on small companies are offered for $29. A free newsletter is obtainable covering small cap investing.

Small Cap Center.com

Like its name, the Small Cap Center is a chock full of small cap
news. Throughout the site there are articles and articles on a multitude of small cap companies. Industry news covering business on
a micro and macro level makes for an interesting and educational
read. An article labeled "China: Embracing Capitalism and Free
Markets" could lead an investor to surmise that it might now be
the time to be in penny stocks poised to do business with the most
populated country in the world. "Online Gambling Still Legal"
discusses how the House failed to pass a bill making online gambling illegal. Investors who fled online gambling stocks might now
start returning if they believe that the bill is truly dead. You would
be well advised to read between the lines of the article to see if the
bill is dead for good or if they will try to pass a revised bill in the
future.

I give this site a very strong rating in their selection and compilation of articles pertaining to small companies.

Trade Idea.com

Compilation of financial links, undervalued opportunities, Internet
trading tips, investment newsletter, and a book store.

AllStocks.com

Links for an alphabetical complete listing of all Over The Counter
Bulletin Board stocks, top ten stocks, active stocks, charts, news,
companies to watch, penny stocks, message boards, market makers,
investment books, real time news pages, and stock picks. You can
build your page on their site. You can label your site and post your
stock picks on it. Investors will come and check your pages and
email you with questions and opinions on your stock picks. Setting
up a page is a great way to meet and discuss stocks with other investors. There are over 20 pages set up by investors on their site.

Yahoo! Finance

The first and largest Internet portal of its kind is Yahoo. Yahoo has a done a meticulous job of providing practical information and functional capabilities. The finance section of the search engine is Yahoo! Finance. The site provides Research: by industry, historical quotes, stock screener, up/downgrades, and SEC filings.

US Markets: Major U.S. Indices, IPOs, Market Digest, and Mutual Funds.

Editorial: The Motley Fool, TheStreet.com, Individual Investor, Wordlyinvestor, Forbes.com, and the Industry Standard.

The quote section is unique among all sites for its collecting power. Upon entering a stock, and the following works for all reporting OTC stocks, you are presented with a detailed quote. The detailed quote is comprised of a box subdivided into the price of the last trade, change percentage wise, previous close, volume, dividend date, day's range, bid and ask, opening price, average volume, 52 week range, earnings per share, P/E, market cap, dividend per share, and the dividend yield.

On the top of the quote box you will find the full name of the company and separate links for news mentioning the company, company's profile, insider transactions, and options. Yahoo will only provide a link when they have the appropriate information for the company. Many companies that are simply shells will not have any news or profile links. The same would apply to a company that does not have active operations and may be investigating new business opportunities. The company might only consist of a CEO who is charting out a new strategy. Once the CEO embarks on a new course he will start to publicize his company, but until then he will most likely devote his time to developing a business and not have the time or resources to keep the outside world enlightened.

At the bottom of the page you will find a listing of all recent articles mentioning the company. A majority of the articles will be press releases that the company has issued to update their investors and potential investors on corporate developments. The articles usually date back for the last 30 days. You can directly contact the company you are researching to obtain older articles.

Small companies are very private about disclosing information due to competitive pressure. Companies will try to only disclose the minimum information required by the SEC so they can still keep proprietary information secret form their competitors. At the same time management of these firms realize that if they want to attract investor interest they are going to have to supply enough information to convince investors like ourselves to call our broker and use our hard earned money to buy shares in their company. The balance that management tries to find leads them to issue allot of general information while at the same time being purposefully vague about other aspects of their business. So what is an investor to do if he is trying to grasp what the essence of the company is?

She will click on the Yahoo profile for the company. When the profile opens up you will find a compilation of public information. There will be a general overview of the company, contact information including the address for corporate headquarter, names and titles of top officers of company with their salaries, and a financial summary of the company. There should be a link for the company's website, and ownership information.

Ownership information will include the percentage of the company owned by the insiders and institutional investors. The profile will note if there has been any change in the percentage of ownership by management and institutional investors.

As part of the profile there is a numbers section entitled Statistics at a Glance. Statistics at a Glance provides a detailed breakdown of all financial information for the stock. This section is fantastic for investors who want to capitalize on undervalued opportunities. How many investors know the cash per share that the company holds? Or the book value of a stock they are investigating? You can look up both of those figures in this section. The section is subdivided into-

Price and Volume: 52 week high and low, recent price, beta, daily volume 3 month and 10 day average.

Stock Performance: 26 week change, 26-week change relative to the S&P 500.

Share-Related Items: Market capitalization, shares outstanding, float.

Dividends and Splits: Annual dividend, last split.

Per-Share Data: Book value, earnings, sales, cash.

Valuation Ratios: Price/book, price/earnings, price/sales.

Income Statements: Sales, EBITDA, income available to common.

Profitability: Profit margin, operating margin.

Fiscal Year: Fiscal information.

Management Effectiveness: Return on assets, return on equity.

Financial Strength: Current ratio, debt/equity, total cash.

Short Interest: Shares short.

You should always make sure to check out the profile of the company you are considering investing in before you place a buy order. Red flags you want to beware of are insiders selling out, heavy institutional selling, a large float, and lack of cash. Profiles are updated as new information is released so it pays to call the company to find out if any numbers have changed. The SEC mandates that they release information to investors so insist and remind them of their obligation. Before you try to the bad cop method, it always pays in the long run to first try to develop a diplomatic approach. If they still do not release the information, and your good manners are not producing results, wish them the best and let them know that they can expect a call from the SEC any day now.

Freerealtime.com

Freerealtime.com provides delayed and real time quotes. This site is a must for any traders who plan on buying and selling penny stocks throughout the day. You must register for real time quotes. Real time quotes will give you the last trade, tell you if the trade was an up tick or down tick, and give you the exact current bid and ask. Most sites have a 20-minute delay, which is too long when you want to actively trade penny stocks. You can also see the pre opening quotes for your selected stocks. If market makers are receiving a large volume of orders for a particular stock before the market opens they will adjust their price for the stock accordingly. You want to see the market makers adjusting the price before the market opens so you can determine if people are getting ready to buy or sell the stock. From 9:15 to 9:30 the bid and ask will be changed depending on pre market trading and orders called in by brokers. I strongly recommend that you never place an order before the market opens for this exact reason. Why give the market makers a hint of what you want to do that day. When they receive your order for a large sell they will lower their bid knowing that you want to sell. Since they know you want to sell they will lower their bid so they can pay you less for your shares.

This is the end of the first chapter. You should review the sites previously discussed and bookmark the ones you like on your Internet browser. Be advised that many sites receive compensation from companies so be vigilant when making your decisions.

CHAPTER 5

Financial Fundamentals

A company's financial fundamentals are what the heart of a human being is to a doctor. If we want to analyze the health of a company we need to be able to delve into its inner sanctum and discover what hidden virtues and ailments the company is hiding inside. The process of examining the financials of a company is like opening an old musty treasure chest. We do not know what we will find until we open the treasure chest and retrieve each component. Then each component needs to be examined separately to see what the individual value is before we can ascertain if it has some value when combined with another artifact from the treasure box. We need to understand what each item on the financial statements means and what the effect of it is on the company. I would advise the reader at this point to buy an accounting review book and read up on some of the basic accounting practices. While this is not necessary, you will find yourself more confident when investigating a company and calling management to discuss the financials. If they see that you are serious and understand accounting issues they will usually put you in touch with their in house treasurer or accountant.

The figures you should become familiar with are the PE, Market Cap, Authorized Shares, Outstanding Shares, Float, Average Volume, 52 week high and low, Cash Per Share, Sales Per Share, and Book Value. There are many other financial figures that are important and appear on a balance sheet statement. In my experience while investing in and trading penny stocks the terms that I have provided are the most important ones to know if you want to succeed beyond your expectations.

The PE, or the price earnings ratio, is determined by dividing earnings by the number of shares. You then divide the price of the share by the earnings per share to obtain the PE ratio. For example, if you have 1,000,000 shares outstanding, and the company has earned $500,000 you would have .50 earnings per share. Now you would take the price of the share, let's picks a random $1 price for the example. $1 divided by .50 is 2 so we know that the stock is trading at twice the value of its earnings, giving the stock a price to earnings ratio of 2. Now if this company belonged to the online gambling sector where the average PE of a company is 8 we would know that the company is undervalued. The problem with most penny stock companies is that they either do not have earnings or they are not publicized. If the company does not have earnings yet, make an estimate of what you expect the company to earn once it becomes profitable.

If you anticipate the company to earn $250,000 within 12 months and the company has 10,000,000 shares outstanding, you are expecting the company to earn .025 a share. Then look at the average PE ratio for stocks in that industry. If the average PE ratio is 10 then you know that the stock will be worth .25 once it earns $250,000. If the company earns even more the stock would be worth more proportionally to the average PE. At this point you have established that the stock will be worth .25. Now take a look at the actual price of the stock today. If the stock is trading below .25 then the stock could be considered a good buy. If the stock is trading for over .25 I would stay away unless I was expecting the stock to make more than .025 a share.

You need to factor in the potential gain you expect for the risk you are willing to take. If the stock in the previous example was trading at .22 it would not be a good buy. It would not be a good investment because you would not want to risk your money in a small stock for a dismal 12% when you could obtain that type of a return with an established company. At .05 you might decide that you are willing to take the risk of investing in an OTC stock. If the stock moves to .25 you will have made 500% on your investment. Above all look at other similar OTC stocks and try to determine what PE they are trading for. Since most OTC stocks are still in the development stage, you will often need to use other factors to measure the value of the stock. Non the less you should be able to find a number of OTC stocks with earnings in the same or similar field as the stock you are researching. Sit down with a calculator and figure out at what PE the other OTC stocks are trading at. Average the PE of the stocks and assign a PE to the sector. Use that average PE to analyze the comparative value of your penny stock. Let us say that you found that the average PE for online gambling OTC stocks is 8 and your stocks' PE is 3. You have certainly found a seemingly undervalued penny stock. But before you eagerly call up your broker to place a buy you need to ask yourself a few hard questions.

If the stock is such a great company why is trading for less than other similar stocks? If the PE is so low why aren't other investors buying up the stock? Am I sure that I produced the correct PE for the stock? Did I compute the average PE correctly?

I will answer the above questions for you but you need to make sure that my answers apply to you. Here are the answers you should arrive at in order of the questions. The stock is trading at a much lower PE than other similar stocks because investors are not sure about the ability of the company to continue producing the level of earnings it has now. You are convinced that earnings will grow not slow down. The next question pertains to why other investors are ignoring the stock if it such a great value. The answer is that other investors have not taken the time to analyze the stock. Once they start realizing what the earnings are for the company the stock will skyrocket. The next questions concern your math abilities, if you are unsure that you came up with the right numbers call up the company and discuss your numbers and results with their accountants. Have someone who is familiar with investing check your math for you to double check for any errors. At this point if your answers match up my answers you have discovered a hidden gem that will soon be trounced upon my hordes of investors. What if the company has no earnings? Read on for more financial techniques.

The market cap of a company is the price of a share multiplied by the total number of shares outstanding. If a company has 500,000,000 shares outstanding and a share price of .01 then the market cap would be $5 million. The market cap is important depending on the type of investment strategy you are pursuing. Investors taking the value approach in penny stocks would want companies with very low market caps. A value investor is looking to buy stocks of companies that have been battered and are worth allot more than the market is valuing them at.

National Rehab Properties Inc, NRPI, is a small real estate development company. They are working on real estate projects with 1 to 2 year completion horizons. NRPI has 14,890,000 shares outstanding. The current price of the stock is hovering around .05 giving the company a market cap of $744,500. That means that the market has valued the company at $744,500. Your job is to decide if the company is worth more than what the market values it. This company has no current earnings so you will have to use another method. The latest press for NRPI stated that they are working on a project with expected sales of $10 million and a $3 million profit. The project should be completed by 2002, or two years from now. Upon successful completion of the project the company will have earnings of $3 million before further expenses. Now we need to go back to the total market cap of the company. If the stock remains at .05 NRPI will have a market cap smaller than its profits. It does not take a veteran trader to realize that investors will buy up the stock until the market cap reflects the value of the company. It is safe to say that if the company produces $3 million in earnings, or .20 a share, the stock will be worth allot more than .05. But how much more will the stock be worth? Look at the market cap of other real estate development companies. Try to find a real estate development company with earnings close to $3 million and a similar segment and see what their market cap is. ABC Real Estate Corp. has earned $3 million for the last three years and has had a sustained market cap of $10 million for the last 5 years. That tells you that a real estate development company with $3 million in earnings should have a market cap of $10 million. Now look two years ahead, NRPI is now earning $3 million and has a market cap of $10 million like its colleagues in the real estate development market. A $10 million market cap represents a 1300% increase from a market cap of $744,500. The key is finding companies that are in the same business segment as your target stock. In addition the above figures depend on the company earning a $3 million profit and other factors that can affect the stock remaining positive. A turn for the worse in the economy would discourage real estate buyers and real estate investors.

There have been episodes of companies being on the verge of going bankrupt. Investors flee the company while the debt collectors knock on the doors of the CEO's office. Rumors of Chapter 11 are leaking out across every message board. Resignations from the corporate suite are a dime a dozen. A temporary secretary is taking all calls and the only information she can provide is that she will be passing on the information to someone who can answer your questions. Early one Monday morning a PR is sent out informing investors that the company is considering entering bankruptcy protection due to its inability to make debt payments. Investors dump the stock in masses driving down a $1 stock to .12 in one month. This is exactly what took place with QDXC a couple of months ago. The stock is now trading at .07 giving the company a market cap of about $80,000. Sure, the company deserves the market cap, it is going bankrupt and soon will be liquidated to pay off the debts owed to its creditors. What do I think of the company?

I love it! Have I lost my mind? No, I have followed company developments carefully. The company has been able to avert bankruptcy by making a deal with its creditors that will keep equity in the hands of stockholders and pay off debt with issued stock.

The bottom line is that the company will remain in business and is even now looking to hire employees. QDXC has averted bankruptcy and is now slowly growing. Try to find another expanding penny stock company with a market cap of $80,000. You could buy 5% of the company with $4,000. If the market cap returns to $1.2 million your 5% stake will be worth $60,000. There are many other companies whose market caps have suffered greatly and are now recuperating.

The key is to use a stock screener and look for public companies with market caps of less than $1,000,000. The stock screener will produce a list of about 25 companies. Using your analytical and research skills shorten the list to 5 companies with attractive business models and markets. Find out why the market caps of those 5 stocks have been reduced and if anything has changed that can reverse fortune of the company. An electronic manufacturer with a new factory will now be able to enter the market and have a product to sell. A bakery that has replaced its old ovens with new machinery can now produce superior quality pastries at a higher volume. Once you have narrowed down the list to two companies, which you feel are changing directions for the better, you can move on to the final step. Compare the two companies to other more established companies. Do the troubled companies on your list have what it takes to enter the market and compete with the more established players? One of the two companies on your list will have a better chance than the other. The correct process to determining which company has the most potential is based on research. The correct research process will be discussed in future chapters.

Authorized number of shares refers to the maximum number of shares a company can issue to the market. The number is written down in its charter. The company can change this number by calling for a shareholder vote to approve changing the number. When a company goes public the corporation indicates how many shares it is authorized to issue. The shares that it issued to the market when it went public are subtracted from the authorized shares.

The remaining number is the additional amount of shares that the company can issue or sell to the market. SSCP has approximately 200 million authorized shares and 19,500,000 shares outstanding. SSCP can issue another 180,500,000 shares to the market. Companies issue more shares when they need to raise funds for operations and for strategic developments.

Stereoscape.com through its subsidiaries, Alpha Sound and Vision, Inc. and American Buyers Club International, Inc. sells high-end audio, video and home theatre equipment through the Internet and its retail outlet in Freehold, New Jersey. The company could issue more shares if it wanted to acquire another company in its line of business. For instance, if SSCP decided that it wanted to sell video equipment in Arizona but lacked the warehouse and distribution channels required, it could look for an acquisition target. SSCP would use its stock to purchase a company in Arizona that already had an operation and distribution operation. It would be easier to buy an existing operation for stock than to use cash to buy a warehouse and pay salaries for new workers. If the new acquisition does not work out favorably the company is only out the stock it issued. If SSCP had tried to start an Arizona operation from scratch it could stand to lose hundreds of thousand of dollars if the venture fails. By issuing stock its downside is limited to the cost of relinquishing an equity position to an outsider.

An investor should be concerned with the size of the authorized shares. If the authorized shares are 10 times the size of the outstanding number of shares the investor could find his position diluted if the company issues more shares. An investor in SSCP would hold 10% of the float if he owned 1.95 million shares. His ownership stake would be cut in half if SSCP issues another 19 million shares. His position would be greatly reduced if SSCP issued 100 million shares.

How do you avoid that situation? You would call the management of SSCP and ask them what their intentions are as far as issuing shares. You would want to know if they plan on issuing more shares to the public and when. If the company tells you that they plan on issuing more shares to in the near future I would be very wary unless I felt that even with the additional shares the value of the stock would rise. For example, if SSCP was to acquire a company that would add earnings of .05 per share it might be worth having my position diluted. The value of the rising stock would offset the loss due to share dilution. To avoid any risk of share dilution invest in companies that have most of their shares issued so you know exactly how many shares to expect in the market.

Outstanding shares are the number of shares that have already been issued on the open market. Outstanding shares include shares that can be freely traded and restricted stock. Restricted stock is shares that have been given to an insider or used in an acquisition. The restricted shares cannot be traded for a minimum of one year and depending on the type of restriction even longer. All stock held by insiders in a company is restricted shares and becomes vested after a certain period of time. The same applies to shares received by a company bought with stock or a consultant compensated with stock. The number of outstanding shares is a public figure provided by public companies upon request and accessible through most financial sites.

The float of a company is the outstanding stock minus any restricted stock. SSCP might have 19.5 million shares outstanding but if 5 million of those shares have been used to pay for an acquisition then they are restricted. The true number of outstanding shares would then be 14.5 million. When contemplating buying stock in a company you want to focus on companies with low floats. Lower floats mean that there is less of a supply of the stock. Like any product that is sold in the open market the rules of supply and demand take place. A scarcity of supply will dictate a higher price when the demand picks up. Buy a stock with only 100,000 shares in the float and you can be assured that any rush of buying will push up the price of the stock. Market makers will not be able to supply stock to the public because of the scarcity of stock available on the market. As the demand increases and the supply is low the price will continue increasing. If the float is 10 million it will take allot more buying to move the price of the stock than if the float is only 1 million presuming that in both instances the price of the stock is the same.

By focusing on stocks with small floats you can be buy a larger percentage of the float and reap the rewards when large amounts of buying pour in. Keep in mind that it a stock with a smaller float will also suffer from more acute price decreases when the selling starts.

Stocks with smaller floats are susceptible to manipulation so you need to beware. A group of individuals can buy up 90% of the float and promote the stock through bulletin boards and message boards. When people try to buy the stock the price will shoot up since the group holds most of the stock in the float. The price will quickly rise convincing many investors that something big is taking place with the company, when the price rises the group of investors will dump their shares on to the unsuspecting investors. The time to buy stocks with small floats is not when you see them promoted on message boards or newsletters. The time to buy the stock is when you find it on your own and the stock has not been discovered yet. You have the most potential when you buy a stock that the majority of investors are not aware of. Once the company starts issuing press releases and attracting investors you will be the one holding the shares that investors will want.

The size of the float is relative to the price of the share. A stock with a float of 200,000 is not small if the price of each share is $20. A float of 10,000,000 is considered small if the share price is .01. Your ability to buy a significant portion of the float will determine whether you consider it small. Keep in mind what the average investors buying power is. Most penny stock investors will invest on average $2,000 in a penny stock. Figure if 100 investors become interested in a company they have the buying power of $200,000. The close the value of the float is to $200,000 the easier it will be for investors to buy up the entire float. The price will rise exponentially if investors try to buy up the entire float a few times over. You do not need me to tell you what would happen if 100 bidders were interested in a lot with an opening bid of a dollar. The price of the lot would explode from one dollar to 20 dollars in no time as each bidder gets caught up in the auction frenzy. The same can happen when there are investors who want to buy stock that is in limited supply. The market maker will keep raising the price and investors will continue raising the prices they are willing to buy the stock at. Within a few hours the stock could be up 50% to 200%.

The message is to always concentrate on stocks with small floats or floats with a low dollar value. The rules of supply and demand will be that much stronger the smaller the supply.

Adding the volume of each of the last 30 trading days together and then dividing the result by 30 compute the Average volume of a stock. You can compute the average volume on an annual basis and for any period you want. The average volume figure is very important for penny stock investors. Volume has a profound effect on all penny stocks. Large volume consisting of selling will drive the price down while large volume consisting of buying will cause the price to increase. The difference between penny stocks and large stocks is that pennies are more susceptible to volume than larger stocks.

Investors will notice an increase in volume and react according to the direction of the price. Like investors in larger companies, penny stock investors are prone to following the flock. When they see a great deal of volume they suspect that a dramatic event has taken place. If they see selling they assume that the event was negative even before checking out to see what the event was. Large volume attracts investors like bees to honey. They gather around and try to decide if people are getting in or out. If they see that investors are rushing in to a stock they assume that something good is going to happen and they join up by buying the stock.

You can take advantage of the herd mentality by predicting the large volume. How do you predict the large volume? By looking at the average volume of a stock compared to its current volume you can see patterns building up. If you notice that the volume has been higher for the last 5 days than it has been on average for the last 30 days and the price is slowly increasing it means that investors are accumulating the stock.

US Homecare Corporation, or USHO was dormant for over 6 months. There had been no trading in it besides an occasional 1000 share trade. The stock had been trading for under .005 for the last few months. One evening I noticed that there had been 80,000 shares bought that day. I could not see a reason for the purchase. I looked at the trading for the last few days and noticed that the day before someone had bought 45,000 shares. Compared to an average volume of 1,000 shares this volume was clearly abnormal. I decided to buy the stock the next day in anticipation of some news. I bought the stock at .007 and sold it two days later for .02. The run did not end there, the stock climbed to .30 within three weeks. If I had been more patient my $5,000 investment could have been worth $200,000 in 15 days. Fortunately there are many more opportunities that present themselves on a daily basis to those who know how to look for them.

The 52-week high and low is the price of the stock at it lowest and highest during the last 52 weeks. This period is important because it covers a full year of trading. Many patterns that repeat themselves will become apparent over the 52-week period. In addition the period serves as a gauge of the value of the stock. A stock with a high of $2 and a low of .09 would be considered a potentially good buy the close the price is to the low. The stock has plenty of room to resume moving up since the price is close to the 52-week low. Investors will feel comfortable buying up the stock as long as it is below the high since they will deem it a good value. The stock will seem to be trading at a discount as long as the price is below the high.

The other approach is to buy stocks whose price has sustained a price higher than its previous 52-week high. The stock can be making another 52-week high if you notice that the stock stays above the last high for a few trading days. This strategy is fraught with risk. Stocks are prone to being sold off when they reach their 52-week highs because investors feel that the stock has reached the highest it can go. The stock can continue climbing if there enough new investors who buy in and offset the selling form the older investors. If the older investors decide not to sell, due to a great piece of news, or fantastic business opportunity, the stock can break out and establish new highs in the coming weeks.

When trying to assign a value to a stock one of the factors to look at is the cash per share that the company has. The cash per share is a public number you can find by going to Yahoo Finance and looking at the profile for the company. You should be able to see how much cash per share the company has. Many companies that are stumbling have large cash reserves from previous operations. A company's current strategy may be faltering because of a termination of a contract. Although the company no longer has the contract it may still have a cash reserve of $1,000,000 from earnings derived while servicing the contract. The $1,000,000 could be used to secure additional contracts to increase its earnings. The cash reserve could be used to start another business or to acquire an existing business. Cash is the most valuable asset a company can have due to its liquidity. If the above company has 1,000,000 shares outstanding it would have cash per share of $1. Many companies in this situation are trading for under their cash value since investors ignore the cash at hand and focus on the short-term situation of the company. The experienced investor knows that company is an attractive acquisition target. Any acquirer can buy the company for .50 and use the cash per share for further business ventures. It would be like going to the bank and withdrawing $1000 for only $500. A problem would arise when the company is facing financial troubles and it will have to use the cash to pay debts. In that situation the cash could easily evaporate as the company struggles to meet its liabilities.

Sales per share are the sales of the company divided by the number of shares. The lifeblood of the company is its sales.

One valuation method is to value a company by the multiples of sales it sells for. At .25 sales per share a .50 stock is selling for twice its sales. Compare that number to other stocks in the same field and see which stock sells for a lower sales multiple. The stock with the lower sales multiple would be considered a better value according to this criterion. Many penny stocks do not have sales so you will need to use alternate methods to compute the value of the stock such as size of the float, market cap, book value, and potential PE.

The intrinsic value of the company is its book value. Subtracting the liabilities from the assets and then dividing that amount by the number of shares measures the book value of a company. When buying a penny stock you need to put yourself in the shoes of a buyer who is buying the company. The closer you can act to a buyer of a retail store the better you will do. A buyer of a retail store takes count of the inventory. He assigns the equipment a value and combines that value with the price of the merchandise. The buyer would then subtract the money owed by the store from the value of its assets and arrive at the value of the store. This value does not take into account goodwill, reputation, customers, or location of the store. The value is only the cost of the physical assets minus any obligations the store has. You need to look at a small company the same way the potential buyer is looking at the store he is considering buying. Instead of having to spend your days sitting over all of the company's financials you can obtain this information from most financial research web sites including Yahoo Finance.

Once you have that number you will have the book value of the company. Try to find companies selling for less than their book values. You are buying those companies for less than their book value worth. In effect you are buying a million dollar business at a discount. Try buying an established profitable business for less than its book value. There are times when a company that was close to failing reverses its course and returns to profitability. The price of the stock has not adjusted to the new fortunes of the corporation.

You can buy the stock while it is still selling at a relative discount to its value. Once investors return to the stock they will bid up the price to an appropriate book value multiple. A profitable company will sell at a minimum of twice of its book value. If you can buy the stock for less than its book value you have the potential to double your money.

Another benefit of buying a company when its stock trades below its book value is its safety. If the company was to be liquidated it would have enough assets to pay off creditors and have money left over for shareholders. A company with more assets than liabilities has a positive net worth. It can always sell assets to pay off debts and still have assets left over. A company in this situation could have a building valued at $400,000 and equipment valued at $50,000. The company would owe $300,000 to its suppliers, $100,000 in wages, and $5,000 in trade association dues. The company has total assets of $450,000 and liabilities of $405,000. The book value of this company is $45,000. If the company has 100,000 shares outstanding the book value per share is .45 per share. Now what if the company announced that they are not sure if they will be able to continue selling tobacco products due to new government regulations? Investors would take this as a bad sign since in this situation the company derives 100% of its revenues from the sale of tobacco products. The stock would be sold driving the price down until the company issues news that things are not as bad as they seem. So for the next 4 days alarmed investors drive down the price from $1 a share to $.20 until the weekend freezes the wave of selling. Investors go home fuming over their losses and wonder how things could have gone so wrong with such a promising company. Then the lawyers for the company review the legislation and discover a loophole. They can still sell their products as long as they package their products with warning labels. The marketing manager determines that consumers will continue buying tobacco products regardless of warning labels. The CEO is overjoyed at the positive reports from his legal and marketing staff. He rushes back to his office where he sends out a press release to the business wires announcing that his business plans on continuing to sell tobacco products and expects higher profits due to the other suppliers that will have to leave the business.

What effect do you think that announcement would have on the price of the company's stock? The price will rise now that the company is back in business. But the price will have its largest rise when investors realize that the stock is trading at way below its book value. Remember, the stock has a book value of .45 and is trading at .20. Once investors realize that the company is now going to head back towards producing profits they will buy back in. The stock will remain a bargain for as long as the stock trades for under .45. You have a guaranteed 150% return waiting to happen.

Find stocks trading for under their book values by using stock screeners. You can request a list of stocks trading at a multiple of their book value. You enter the multiple you want and the stock screener will produce a list of stocks matching the criteria. I found AHIC by doing a search on Hoovers' stock screener. I selected stocks trading for under .50 of their book value. I scrutinized the list of companies and found a small medical practice company. At the time that I purchased AHIC they owned 5 clinics and were trading at .03 a share. The stock climbed to .15 as their financials improved and investors realized the value of the assets the company possessed.

I called the company and spoke to the CEO who told me that his company was not facing bankruptcy and was in the process of selling unprofitable clinics to shore up its financial health. I looked at the assets that the company had and realized that the company could afford to sell off some its assets to pay off debt and still remain with assets.

Make sure to compare to the book value of the stock with the book value of other companies in the same business segment. Just because your stock has a price to book value multiple of .10 does not meant the stock is a good value. A company in an industry that has become obsolete is not a good value under any conditions.

CHAPTER 6

Corporate Developments

There are over 6500 securities trading on the OTC BB market and on the pink sheets. Finding the right penny stock to invest in can seem very difficult. This chapter will provide a list of corporate developments you should look for to help you select profitable investment opportunities. The following corporate developments when combined with other criteria discussed in the book will lead you to find stocks that have the potential to rapidly increase in price.

Businesses in every market and of every size share one similarity. They all depend on the people running them. The management of the company must be well versed in the product or service that the company sells. Since every company has to sell its product at some point the fortune of the company will depend on the ability of management to sell. The executives of the corporation must have a strong belief that their product is unique. Costumers will pick up on the confidence of the executives in their product. Orders for the product will only be placed if the executives standing behind the product seem professional and capable of ensuring delivery of a quality product. The image the executives portray will mean more than all the advertising the company can do.

A great deal rests on the capabilities of the corporate suite. The company depends on the drive and leadership of the CEO. He must serve as a motivator and visionary for his employees. The middle level managers need to be loyal to the company. They need to work just as hard when the company faces obstacles as when it is prospering.

Investors will sense if the management of a company is taking charge and aggressively pursuing the business plan of the company. Investors know that corporate leaders can grow a two-employee business 10 times its size if they have the drive and business acumen.

The problem arises when management is no longer efficient. This problem could be caused by many factors that are not always in the control of the present management. A CEO of a commercial printer can run into trouble facing competition because of his inability to grasp the latest technological changes in the printing industry. The treasurer of a small clothing manufacturer might be having personal problems that limit his involvement in the affairs of his company. There are many reasons why the current management of a company might find itself unable to run the company efficiently. The corporate boards will usually try to remedy the situation by bringing in new executives to the company who are familiar with the latest technology or have a clear grasp of the nature of the company's business.

Every day there is an announcement by another company that it is changing its corporate suite. Companies with a new management have the potential to excel in their field. The new executives arrive at the company with vigor and excitement. They have accepted the challenge of working at a small company because they realize the potential that is only found at a small growing business. The company can use the connections from their previous jobs. An executive leaving a large oil company to work for a small refinery will know many of the players in the oil market. He can use his connections to obtain a cheaper distributor for his new employer. Or he can flip open his Rolodex and start calling on old customers to convince them to use the service of his new employer. The opportunities presented by new executives are limitless as long as the new executive is properly compensated. Equity compensation will ensure that the new executive is motivated to bring up the price of the stock. Most small companies need to offer equity positions to lure Vice Presidents of established companies to make the leap and work for a smaller company.

After reading about the new management hired by the company investigate their credentials. Look at their degrees and job experience. Where have they worked and for how long? Would you hire that individual to run your company? Is the individual appropriate for the position? Call the company and ask to speak to the new executive. Be polite and express your interest and position. She will appreciate that investors have noticed her being hired and are interested in getting to know her. Have questions ready since her time will be precious and she might not have more than 10 minutes to talk.

You should walk away feeling confident in the new executive the company has hired. Companies with new management are worth investing since now they have executives who can continue expanding the company.

Part of hiring a new executive is the prestige and the respect that the individual brings with him. Companies will often invite a well-known individual to sit on their board. By inviting a popular individual to sit on your board you lend your company prestige. The company attains legitimacy by having an authority in the field join the company. Picture a small chocolate factory hiring the retired CEO of Hershey as its new CEO. People in the chocolate industry would conclude that the small chocolate company must have something very special going for it or otherwise they could not have hired one of the top individuals in the chocolate industry. Customers would be attracted to this new company since they would believe that the CEO would instruct the small company on the proper techniques of chocolate production. Suppliers would be willing to extend credit based on the trust they would have for the new CEO. He did not run Hershey by being dishonest to his suppliers. Suppliers would race to sell products to the company since they know that which ever supplier is selected would have the implied approval by one of the industry leaders in the business. After having the ex CEO of Hershey as client customers will knock down their doors to be supplied by them.

How does the hiring of the ex CEO of Hershey affect investors? That chocolate company will now be the talk of the industry. The name of the company will make the headlines, attracting new investors and customers to the company. The company will increase its earnings through its new customers. Higher earnings will mean a higher stock valuation. Investors will also buy the stock based on the name of the new CEO.

The same would apply to a penny stock company that invited a known politician to sit on its board. Many past Congressmen sit on the boards of small companies. They can lend their experience from working in the government to the small company. The respect that their names carry opens doors that would otherwise remain closed to the small company. Board members are often compensated with stock in the company. The Congressman or potential board member will strenuously investigate the character of the company he is contemplating joining. She does not want her name tarnished if the small company later becomes embroiled in fraud. For that same reason once a former Congresswoman decides to sit on the board of a company investors take the acceptance of the seat as a tacit approval of the company.

A long-term indicator of the prospects of a company is whom they have been able to hire and convince to sit on their boards. An important executive in the communications industry does not want to disappear into oblivion by working for a small company that will fade into the background. Once the aspiring executive decides to work for the company it is because he knows that the company's product is innovative and will cause waves in the industry. He is staking the welfare of his career on the success of the company. Once he leaves his employer to work for a small company he runs the risk of being black listed. His former employer will resent the fact that he has taken the experience and contacts he developed to another company. The doors of his former employer will be sealed for good. The executive better know what he is doing before he makes the leap. That is the reason when a well known executive does decide to work for a penny stock company, we can ascertain that the company has a great deal of potential. You can be sure that the company will not remain a penny stock for long.

Oxford-Knight recently announced the signing of Vanna White as major Shareholder and Consultant & Advisor of their Subsidiary "SeeUatHome.Com". Hiring a world-renowned TV celebrity as a consultant will lend prestige to the company. Her name will carry weight when OKTI looks for media exposure. The company should be able to reach out to the circle of friends and acquaintances that Vanna White developed in working in the TV industry. Some of those friends might be fellow actresses who would be willing to endorse the company's web site. The added publicity from having Vanna White as a member of the company will attract many investors who would not have other wise heard of the stock. You can be sure that the press release announcing her affiliation with the company stood out from the other hundreds of press releases issued that day.

Retired military officials are also very beneficial to companies. They keep in touch with the officers they served with. They know the names of the people who make the decisions. A company seeking to obtain a waste disposal contract from the Navy would benefit greatly by having a retired admiral on its board. The admiral would know who to call in the Navy procurement office. The officer in charge of procurement for the Navy would respect and trust the admiral's advice. The procurement officer might also be hoping to obtain a job at the company upon his retirement from the Navy. The procurement officer would not assign the contract to the company nor would the retired admiral ask for it unless the company was capable of delivering. Many board members do resign their positions after discovering that the company cannot deliver on its promises. Therefore, you still need to investigate a company regardless of who sits on the board. You do not want to buy a stock only to hear the next day that a board member has resigned.

Over seas markets offer many opportunities that are not found domestically. Labor is cheaper in many countries than it is in the

United States. Minimum wage in the United States is over $5 an hour while the average Mexican worker earns $4 a day. Lower labor costs translate into lower production costs. An American sweater manufacturer can produce hand made sweaters for a tenth of the cost that it would cost him to produce the same sweaters in the United States.

The largest obstacle to over seas production in the past had been the inferior quality of goods. Asian factories could export watches to American wholesalers cheaper than the American manufacturers could produce them for. Two weeks after selling the watches the wholesalers would receive a significant percentage of them back. The quality was inferior and often the watches would simply stop working. Retailers complained and insisted on better merchandise even if the cost was higher. The over seas factories hunkered down and decided that they would not relinquish this lucrative market. Quality control became a priority for the manufacturers. Shipments sold better and suffered less returns. Soon the notion of poor quality goods disappeared. Today, the quality of overseas goods is on par with American produced goods.

Many small micro cap companies are starting to take advantage of over seas production. The management of the company realizes that in order to compete with other suppliers of their product they need to keep costs down. They travel overseas and find out that they can produce the same VCR they make now for 40% less. They contract with a factory and split the savings with the consumer. Management knows that they can now lower the price by 20% and still make an extra 20% profit on each unit. The small company will not increase its earnings by 20% without having to sell a single more item than it sold the previous year. At this point consumers will start be drawn to this VCR manufacturer because its cheaper prices. The end result will mean higher sales to more customers and a higher profit margin on each unit. Earnings are what investors look for. The VCR manufacturer will have higher earnings per share thus increasing the value of the stock. Look for companies announcing a move of their productions to overseas facilities.

Another benefit of operating over seas is the untapped consumer market. A majority of the houses in this country have phone
service. Every rural and inner city neighborhood has public phones.
Access to a phone in this country is not even an after thought in
this country. The story is very different in third world countries.
Most people do not have phone service in their homes nor have
access to a public phone. This situation has created a great demand for phone service in developing countries. Due to the high
cost of building the necessary infrastructure people are turning to
cellular technology. The cost of setting up cellular operations is
significantly cheaper than line based phone service, especially in
dense jungle areas that can only be reached by foot.

Many penny stock companies are specializing in providing
telecommunication services to areas that lack phone service. ADGI
is hard at work to develop a communication network to provide
phone service in South America and other areas of the world.

There is a great demand for many products over seas that are
staple goods in this country. Micro cap companies that decide to
embark on the pursuit of international opportunities can reap the
rewards that come from small to zero competition. Keep an eye
out for companies that have announced that they will start selling
their product or service to an overseas market. The price of ADGI
stock rose from a low of one cent to over .25 after announcing their
international expansion.

Products that are in high demand overseas are clean water,
vitamins for under nourished populations, communication technology, computer equipment, Internet technology, and clothing.
Call companies dealing in these products and ask them if they
have any plans on selling to over seas markets. The best time to
buy into the stock is before everyone else knows that the company
is selling over seas. Once the announcement is made you will have
a much shorter time to decided if you should buy the stock or not.
Try to research companies to determine which ones will be selling
over seas and then call the company and confirm if they do have
international plans.

Lucrative markets are also found domestically. The lucrative markets might not always be the most glamorous. Everyone knows how much money there is to be made in developing a new drug. But how many of us know that there profits to be made in providing a sanitary product that will be used in every public bathroom.

The Hydrogiene Corp. manufactures and markets the Hydrogiene family of personal care systems that convert tank-type and flush-type valve toilets into personal multi-functional cleansing, water therapy and sitz bath systems. The Company's systems are similar in function to Europe's bidets without the additional plumbing and space requirements. The Company's products are the Theraclenze and Mediclenze systems, which are European-style personal hygiene and water therapy systems for tank-type or flushometer-equipped toilets. These systems may be installed on existing toilets without incurring additional plumbing, electrical or construction costs.

The demand for cleaning systems for public toilets will only increase as the public becomes more educated concerning the diseases and health hazards associated with public facilities. HICS has entered a market with no major competition. The market rewarded the company by bringing up its stock from .04 to as high as $2 in three months. The stock has settled in the .40 range delivering a 1000% return to investors who bought in at .04.

Companies that enter a new market have the potential of capturing a niche before the competition wakes up and sees the opportunity. Companies that enter an untapped market or segment of a larger market should be considered very attractive by investors who are looking to reap great rewards from penny stock investing.

Two approaches can be taken to determine a course of action. You can either anticipate markets that will become hot and see who can serve them best, or you can wait for companies to announce that they will be entering a new market. The first approach would require reading the daily newspapers, watching the CNBC, and listening to Bloomberg radio. Your aim is to discover new markets or business segments before other people do. You might listen to Bloomberg radio cover a story on the changing dietary needs of aging athletes. You would then research which companies could supply the aging athletes with the best nutritional supplements. Call the company and ask them if they will be selling to that segment of the market. If they plan on servicing that segment the company will profit from operating in an over looked niche.

The other approach is more reactive to news. This method would rely on companies ending out press releases. You would look on a daily basis for press releases announcing a company operating in a new market. The ideal press release would be from a company announcing that they will now be selling nutritional supplements to aging athletes. The press release would go on to explain how the market is worth $500 million and there are no companies focusing solely on these consumers. If the company can capture 2% of the market they would have sales of $10 million. Now it all depends on the management's ability to service that market. If they capture an even percentage of that market you could be sitting on future big board company.

Along with a new market segment, operating in a new geographical area can be just as lucrative. The market in a metropolitan area might be saturated with fast food stores. But if the fast food operator expands into rural towns he will find many willing consumers. Rural towns are underserved because of their lesser economic potential. The rules of business dictate that you would rather capture .001% of a 12,000,000 -customer base than 5% of a 1000 customer base. But what if you could capture 100% of a 1000 -customer base?

Many rural towns do not have any fast food stores. By opening up a fast food store you can serve those customers every time they want to eat outside of the home. What if you opened up the only fast food store in 10 different rural areas? You would have a virtual monopoly in those 10 rural areas.

There are many companies expanding into underserved areas. By investing in those companies you can capture the benefits of owning a business with a monopoly on its product. The same benefits would apply to a clothing retailer opening up the first clothing store in a new mall down in Laredo, Texas. The retailer would have the opportunity of selling clothing with only competition from mom and pop clothing shops. Focus on companies entering geographical areas that are underserved where the company can enjoy a virtual monopoly on its product.

A micro cap company needs to distinguish itself from its competition. This can be an arduous task for any small company that shares vendors with other competitors. A computer reseller that resells the same computers as its competition will have to beat out the competition based on price. If the reseller focuses on price to win customers it is entering a very harmful cycle. Every time it lowers its price its competitors will respond by lowering their prices. This price war cycle has led many businesses into ruin. Then what can a company do to stand out from the crowd? It needs to sell another product. The company will have to reach out to another supplier and form an exclusive agreement to be the only party authorized to sell the product to a particular market. Many large companies appoint agents to sell their products to markets that they do not serve. IBM can develop a program for chicken farmers to manage their farms. The executives at IBM do not know anyone in the farming business so they form an agreement with a farming consulting group. IBM will grant an exclusive license to the consulting group to sell the program. The consulting group promises IBM that they will see 1,000 programs annually and slowly introduce other IBM products in exchange for the exclusive right to sell the program and future farming software to the industry.

This arrangement is very common among large corporations that have developed products for smaller markets. The large corporation might find it to expensive to set up a sales operation for the smaller market. Instead of having their own sales force preoccupied to sell to the farmers in this case, they contract out the work to another company. Long Distance companies often hire marketing groups to sell their service. The marketing group receives a residual commission on all customer bills in exchange for selling the service.

Penny stocks that have exclusive arrangements with well-known corporations are poised to reap tremendous gains. A reseller for IBM software can use the clout of selling an IBM product to sell the software. The reseller will have an opportunity to introduce other programs while he sells the IBM software. He might not have ever gained access into his customers' offices unless he carried the well-known brand. Customers would not have given him a chance if he were another brand X company pushing a generic product. For this reason many micro cap companies look to buy merchandise from major companies for resale purposes. The micro cap company can use the name of its supplier to gain it a foothold in potential customers' doors. Once a micro cap has secured an excusive contract to sell a well-known product it can count on torrents of strong sales. The micro cap company with an exclusive agreement to sell a brand name product will demolish its competition. Customers will always prefer to buy the product with the recognized name as long as the price is reasonable. In addition, when the larger company does its advertising, attention will also be drawn to the micro cap company.

The dream of every small business is to secure one account that will provide millions of dollars in revenues. This dream can be attained by small business with drive and a product that can take the market by storm. Wal-Mart instructs its buyers to seek out new innovative products that it can sell on its shelves. Hundreds of manufacturers compete with each other to showcase their product to the buyers. The manufacturers know what is at stake. If Wal-Mart selects their product they will be placing orders for thousands of units on a monthly basis. If Wal-Mart decides to buy hot sauce from a company it will initially carry it in a test run in 10 of its stores. If the product sells it will order for more stores and keep tabs on its popularity. Once the retail chain decides to make the product as regular the company can count on tens of thousands of dollars of reorders from the chain. A company selling its product to Wal-Mart will have plenty of credibility with other retail chains. The other retail chains that are struggling to keep up with

Wal-Mart will also place orders for the item. Within months the tiny company can find itself selling hundreds of thousand of units on a monthly basis to 3 or 4 retail chains. How many cans of Coke do you think Coca Cola sells to retail chains on weekly basis? The potential for a small company is tremendous if they are able to develop even one large account. Look for companies that have secured a large customer for its product or services. Once they secure one major customers more will follow. The company will soon be forced to expand to meet the demand from its new customers. All it takes is one mention in the newspaper that Motorola will now be purchasing all its copy paper from one penny stock company and the price will escalate before you can reach for the phone and call your broker.

Affiliations are very important. Companies, like individuals, are judged by whom they are affiliated with. The right crowd lends credibility to an individual. A lawyer who keeps the company of judges and government officials would be well regarded by his neighbors. Credibility is lent to an individual based on the people he keeps company with. If the President of the United States decided to spend time with a businessman we would assume that the President is familiar with the character of the man. We would conduct business with the President's friend based on the credibility his friendship with the President would provide. The same situation takes place with companies. We want to know whom they are associated with. Businesses join the Better Business Bureau to show potential customers that they are not fly by night operations. They invite potential customers to call the BBB to verify that they have no complaints lodged against them. The associations a company has will make the difference between attracting and turning away customers.

Penny stocks have the added pressure of proving their credibility. The initial response people give when they hear a penny stock mentioned is that it is a fly by night operation. A large company relies on its investor relations department to keep a positive image. General Motors sponsors athletic events year round to promote its brands. It gives millions of dollars away in charity every year and sponsors scholarships for inner city children. Penny stock companies do not have the resources to sponsor races, donate millions to charity, or provide full scholarships for disadvantaged students. They are faced with an uphill struggle when trying to promote their corporate identity. It is for this reason that affiliations are so important. Micro cap companies need to seek out non-profit organizations to which they can donate services or products. The non-profit organization will recognize the donation by issuing an award. The penny stock company can then send out a press release mentioning the award. People respect companies that donate to charity.

Sponsoring athletic events contributes to the company's image. The sponsor of an athletic race receives publicity from the media that covers the event. The newscaster will repeat a few times throughout the program the name of the sponsor. Every time the camera zooms in on the event the viewers will see the flag announcing the name of the corporate sponsor. Sponsoring athletic events is one of the best ways for a small company to advertise its name at a minimal cost.

Athletic events also build an image of a company. A company that sponsors surfing events will build the image of a hip organization in touch with young people. A corporation sponsoring Basketball games for inner city youth will be seen as benevolent. Companies spend time before selecting an event to match it to the image they are seeking to create.

Penny stocks that sponsor athletic events and non-profit organizations have the opportunity to garner a great deal of publicity in the national media. Try putting on price of the publicity generated when the President of the Red Cross thanks General Motors, Ford, and the micro cap company for sending much needed aid to earthquake victims in Turkey. Every major news station will carry the image of the Red Cross official thanking the micro cap company for its donation. Suddenly the penny stock company is no longer a fly by night operation. Now it is a corporation with the welfare of people on its mind. A reporter arrives at the corporate head quarters to interview the CEO. The CEO is more than happy to explain why he decided to donate 10,000 units of his product to the victims. He will tell the reporter how his product his suitable for the needs of distressed victims all over the world. The next day relief organizations around the world are placing orders for his product. A simple gesture from a penny stock can elevate from obscurity to the limelight. When you see a penny stock make a donation or sponsor an athletic event you can be sure that publicity will follow.

The most direct act that a company can do to elevate the price of its stock is to buy up its own shares in the open market. Companies often launch buy back programs when they seek to diminish the number of outstanding shares. The shares bought in the open market can be retired. Retired shares are no longer counted as outstanding. Investors will value the remaining shares at a higher price. A company with a $2 million market cap that has 4 million shares outstanding would have a per share price of .50. With a corporate buy back of shares the outstanding number of shares would be reduced. Supposing that the company retired 1 million shares the outstanding number would decrease to 3 million. If the market cap remains at $2 million, it has no reason to go down since investors still have the same valuation for the company, each share would now be worth .67, .27 more than they were worth prior to the buy back.

There are a few reasons for instituting a buy back. One reason for a company deciding to buy back its shares is to shore up confidence in the company. Management wants to show investors that they feel that the stock is a good long-term investment. By buying up stock they are showing investors that they feel that the company stock is a good investment. It is one thing for the CEO to announce that his company will increase earnings and it is another thing to put his money where his mouth is and buy up company stock. The CEO will be fired if he buys up company stock with company resources only to see the stock plummet in value.

Investors who see the company buying its own stock realize that management, who is privy to more information than investors, believe in the long term value of their stock.

Corporate management initiates buy back programs to push up the price of its stock. The treasure of the company knows that investors will translate the buying of stock as a positive sign on the value of the stock. Unfortunately, this can be done at investors' expense. A company with no prospects might start buying up stock to push the price of its stock up. As the price goes up the CEO who is sitting on 100,000 shares starts selling his shares into the market a the higher price. The SEC would surly step in if the CEO would act so brazenly. To avoid SEC scrutiny the corporate officer will have a relative buy stock and instruct him to sell it as the price goes up. Investors will interpret the corporate buying of stock as a vote of faith in the value of the stock. While in reality, the CEO only wants the price of the stock to move up so his relative or friend can dump his shares. The profits would then be split between the CEO and the seller of the stock. This fraud is very hard to detect and even harder to prove. To avoid falling victim to this manipulative action call a company to find out why they are buying up their stock. Make sure they can supply a concrete reason for buying the stock. Most companies do not want to invite the wrath of the SEC but it for the few rotten apples in the barrel that you need to watch out for.

PCBM announced a buy back of its shares to reduce the outstanding number of shares. They retired the number of shares making each share worth more. On the announcement alone the stock rose from .10 to .17 in two days before settling at the end of the week at .13. PCBM is involved in the check cashing business and has used its resources to make acquisitions. It clearly believes that its shares will appreciate in value as its acquisitions add profits to the corporate bottom line. By retiring shares, it can later issue them again when they are worth more.

Pinnacle Business Management PCBM announced that it would retire or buy back a total of 105 million shares of its common stock.

In making the announcement, Pinnacle indicated that the transactions are slated to occur progressively over the next six months. That amount of buying itself will push up the price in the long term. That type of buying is the same as 10 investors buying 10 million shares each and agreeing not to sell them for a while. Investors who want to buy the stock in the future will have to deal with a smaller supply than was previously available. The laws of supply and demand will increase the price even if the amount of buying stays steady during the next 6 months due to the diminishing of supply. Positive news would have the added effect of encouraging shareholders to add to their position and for new investors to take a position in the stock. The stock could then sharply rise as the new and old investors are competing for the remaining stock. The one factor that can slow down the rise of the price will be early investors taking their profits as the price goes up. The early investors would need to be convinced by the company that there is more to come in order to encourage them to stay on as shareholders.

Review the corporate developments that have been discussed in this chapter. When you feel that you have a clear grasp on them look for companies that have had those developments. Make notes of the developments that companies undergo and the effect the events have on the stock's price.

CHAPTER 7

Turn Around Situations

A turn around situation is when a company is heading in an adverse direction and manages to reverse course. The company is often geared on a path of financial destruction with no light at the end of the tunnel. It might not be the company's fault that it is headed towards ruin. Outside factors such as lawsuits could spell doom for a company with limited cash reserves. Government regulations can negatively affect what was once a profitable business.

Gun manufacturers are now facing great challenges as the public becomes enraged with the spread of guns. Lawsuits and major boycotts can force many profitable smaller gun manufacturers into bankruptcy. A law dictating that guns can no longer be sold unless they are specifically sporting guns would spell doom for many gun companies. Lets fast-forward a year after the law has passed. American Gun Maker cannot sell its revolver any longer due to the passing of the law. The CEO sadly gathers his employees for a meeting. With tears in his eyes he announces that everyone will be laid off a week from now. The human resources office will help workers find other work. Thanking everyone for their years of devotion he explains how the company cannot sell its hand guns any longer due to the passing of the law.

Word gets out to Wall Street that the company is going to close its doors. Mutual fund managers unload their holdings of American Gun Maker. Brokers start calling their clients to sell the stock. Within a month what was once a $20 stock sells for .50 a share. The CEO sits alone in his office wondering what do now.

He has paid all of corporate debts using the remaining cash. Staring at the desolate factory he thinks what a pity it will be to let all this machinery go to waste. Leaning against an empty crate he thinks of all the machinery that will now be sold for scrap across the country. Then that event that has transformed ordinary men into luminaries strikes him. His imagination starts spinning, moving the wheels in his brain. What if he used his factory to produce armaments for foreign police forces?

A month later the American Gun Manufacturer announces the signing of an agreement to supply the police force of Brazil with 10,000 new revolvers. Wall Street is taken by surprise. The analysts race to delve into this development. A company that they had written off has now returned to the market. The Wall Street Journal wants to know if this comeback is for real. The CEO has his vice president tell the venerable newspaper that not only are they back in business but they have just signed their second contract to supply the Polish police force with 5,000 new semi automatic guns along with enough ammunition to last them for 6 months. Investors start buying up the stock bringing the price back to over $10. Investors who thought that this company could be turn around most likely bought the stock at its lowest, when it traded for .50. They are now sitting on a 2000% gain.

You can take advantage of a turn around situation if you know what to look for. There are opportunities to participate in a turn around situation that are not as drastic as a company facing bankruptcy. Some turn around situations arise from short-term events such as a mistake in the corporate direction the company took. The management of the company could have opened a sales outlet that they had to soon close due to lack of profitability. After investors sell off the stock after blaming management for their incompetence, the stock could be sitting at an attractive price.

Stocks are frequently sold off disproportionately to the loss that a company has incurred. A company that has suffered a 10% drop in their earnings will see a greater percentage drop in the stock price than the percentage of earnings it lost. This happens since investors lose faith in the ability of the company to produce profits. They rationalize that if the company could declare a loss in a good economy it will do terrible as the economy slows. Prices of stocks have dropped in the past as much as 30% on a 10% drop in earnings. The price of this stock could potentially turn around and recover to its prior price if the company declares an increase of earnings the next quarter.

A micro cap company that declares a loss can see its .20 stock tumble to .05 as investors expect the worst and place their hard earned money elsewhere. This is the perfect turn around situation. Chances are that investors have over reacted. The company could have suffered a loss due to a seasonal event. Maybe warm weather slowed sales of the company's jackets. The company still has a large base of repeat customers for its jackets and the same 10 stores that carry them. The only problem was that the warm weather discouraged new purchases of the jacket. As long as the weather next winter is cold the company will return to profitability. If the company does return to profitability the stock could return to .20 quadrupling your money. Beware, since a repeat of warm weather next winter will certainly spell another loss for this company.

A negative event such as bad publicity can also take an excessive toll on the stock's price. The SEC could launch an investigation of an individual who was associated in the past with the company. The specter of an SEC investigation will drive down any stock's price. The SEC will ask for record from the company dealing with the former employee. Bloomberg will most likely do an article on the SEC investigation. Naïve investors will misunderstand and assume that the company is under investigation and sell out. The bad publicity will keep buyers away letting the sellers force down the price with their sales. It is now up to you to decide if the company has done anything wrong or if the SEC is really only concerned with the past employee. You can call the SEC but they will not offer information on any ongoing investigations. The company will try to put a positive spin on the investigation. You are really on your own in this situation. If you can ascertain that the company has not done anything wrong and the SEC is not investigating them, it might be time to buy the stock. When the investigation withers down investors will slowly return to the stock. Once the investigation is out people's minds the price of the stock should return to its prior valuation.

One of my favorite turn around situations is when a stock depreciates in price due to a negative event in another company. This happens when a well-known stock goes down in price. People start selling off similar stocks because they associate the negative event that happened to the well-known stock with their stock. When a large computer company declares a quarterly loss investors will sell off other computer stocks. An online gambling company that is the focus of an investigation will have a negative effect on other online gambling stocks. People will hear about the investigation and sell their online gambling stocks. Stocks in the same sector usually move in conjunction to each other when significant events take place. The logic is that bad news for one stock in the industry is bad news for the rest of the companies in that industry. This logic is true when the event will change the industry. The government issuing excessive restrictions on an industry will affect every company operating in the market. A plane crash will discourage travelers from flying on any airline's airplane regardless of which airline had the accident.

The logic is not correct when the event only affects one particular company. A strike at one package deliverer will not adversely affect other deliverers. A few years ago all employees at UPS went on strike. The stock of UPS suffered do to the business that the company was mission out on. That unfortunate period for UPS delivered a tremendous opportunity for the competition. UPS customers looked hard for other shippers to meet their needs. Many small delivery services gained customers they would have otherwise not had.

The problem is that people sometimes overlook the benefits of a negative event on other companies in the same sector. They sell stocks in the sector without slowing down to strategically look at

the situation. As an advanced investor when you sell a sell off in a
sector you need to enter with your guns blazing. Look over the
stocks that have been sold off and sweep in picking up the stocks
that should not have been sold off along with the other stocks in the
sector. Once the panic subsides investors should buy back the shares
they only sold days ago. The money you spend buying stocks after
other investors wrongly sold them might be the fastest and easiest
money you ever made. When Internet stocks started falling out of
favor I saw many Internet penny stocks fall from the dollar range to
less than .20. Once people started returning to the quality Internet
stocks they started climbing back to their previous prices.

Companies go through different stages in their development.
Like a growing child, they first start out cautiously exploring the
market. As they slowly grow they start expanding into new opportunities that present themselves. They then reach their maturity
age when they have become established and found their path. This
is like an individual having settled into a career and following a set
routine day to day. An individual at this stage of life soon grows
restless and finds the need for change. He wants a change in his
life and is willing to try his luck at another job. Packing up his
bags he might move on to a new city to meet new people and try
out another career. Companies are the same. After many years of
being on the same path they sometimes decide to enter a new
market. The executives will canvass the market for new ideas until
they settle on what seems like a promising idea. The company will
start advertising the new product or service hoping to prosper in
the market. While sometimes companies will be successful the
odds are against them. Their experience lies in another area. Even
though the CEO might have years of experience in the sock business she will still be unfamiliar with the inner workings of the shoe
business. Her company will falter until they reverse course and
return to the business she is experienced in. Many companies
stumble while attempting to enter a new business. The intelligent
ones will soon return to their original business and watch their
coffers become replete with revenue. Opportunity lies in investing

in a company when it has announced that it will be reverting back to its original business line. Traders will take time to react to the news. Profits are made when no one else is looking. Most investors will want solid proof that the company has now returned to profitability and to its original business plan. Once everyone receives the required proof of the company's actions it will be too late to capitalize on the share price. You need to be in when the company decides to turn around. You can then sit back and watch the price rise as investors who become convinced of the company's intentions start buying the stock.

The last stage of a company's life is similar to a person's elderly stage. Ambitions have slowed down. Management has exhausted all growth opportunities. Customers stop placing orders and switch their business to the new entrant to the market. Bills start piling up in the accounts payable department. Employees sit idly by without having any work after the loss of a major client. Sales people jump ship to a more profitable firm leaving the company without an ability to draw new business.

This is the process that leads thousands of old established companies into bankruptcy every year. Meetings are arranged with debtors to settle debts and hopefully find away to avoid liquidation. The debtors propose a reorganization plan in which they would own 80% of the new company leaving management with the remaining 10%. Equity holders would see their stake in the company extinguished since in most bankruptcy re organization cases common equity is voided.

The common stock of Bradley traded as low as .02 after it entered into bankruptcy protection. When the company emerged from bankruptcy the old stock was cancelled making it worthless. New stock was issued to bond holders, debtors, and to the banks. Shareholders in firms facing bankruptcy know that if the company emerges through a re organization plan they will be left holding worthless stock. The closer the company gets to the point of entering a re organization plan the more shareholders will sell their holdings.

Not all bankruptcies end in re organizations. Companies have been able to save themselves from entering bankruptcy proceedings by a last minute suitor. The suitor will lend the company enough money to pay off its debts in exchange for a higher interest rate or an equity position. Or the firm can show the court that they have a new source of revenue to help them pay off their debts. Creditors will be in favor of any plan that allows the company to remain in business if they will have a better chance to recuperate their money. The creditors know that if the company is liquidated they will be lucky to receive ten cents on the dollar. The bondholders are the ones who usually push for a re organization of the company since they know that they will then receive control of the new company.

As long as the company can show that it has a plan to return to profitability the creditors will give the company breathing room. The challenge is to find companies that are headed towards bankruptcy and are able to make the climb back towards profitability. Companies that faced bankruptcy see their stocks trading for as low as 5% of their highs. QDXC faced major financial problems and experienced a drop in its stock from $1.50 to as low as .06. The executives in charge of Quadrax Corp used their connections and business acumen to avoid bankruptcy and initiated a plan to return to profitability. The stock recently rebounded to .16. The company is continuing to make slow but steady progress.

Investing in bankrupt companies is fraught with an even greater risk than investing in penny stocks. I would only suggest investing in the stock of a bankrupt company when it has already started climbing back in price and the company can show that it will avoid liquidation or reorganization. Using this approach you will miss the extra profits you could have had if you bought the stock at its most low. In the long run you will be better off missing the first percentages of profit in exchange for the added security of knowing that the company is back in its feet and returning to profitability.

ITEC, Imaging Technologies Corp, is a worldwide pioneer in the development, manufacturing, licensing and distribution of high-quality digital imaging solutions. The Company produces controllers for non-impact printers and multifunction peripherals, monochrome and color printers, printer controllers, external print servers and software to improve the accuracy of color reproductions.

ITEC reduced its liabilities from $19 million to $13 million since June 30, 1999, and increased its sales backlog to $5 million. The company also signed an agreement for a financing facility providing commitments to purchase up to $36 million of its common shares over the next two years.

The company managed to turn around itself from the brink. With the financing in place and reduction of liabilities the company should be able to focus on its revenue producing operations. The stock market has rewarded the company by pushing up its share price from as low as .19 to as high as .96.

Finding companies being turned around like ITEC is not as hard as it seems. Signs of a turn around can be a press release announcing a new customer or new line of credit. Companies want to attract investors and will do everything they can to inform the public that they have improved their health. Companies that are recuperating from financial perils know that one of the best sources of cash is to sell shares to the public. For the public to want to buy the shares of a company they need to be sold on the company. Management knows that the pressure is on them to regain the confidence of the investment community. They inform their Public Relations firm to send out any good news they have to all the business wires. Skilled PR firms will arrange for articles to be written on their clients in local and national publications. Your job is to read all the articles written and press releases sent out by the companies and decide which company has the best chance of turning itself around.

CHAPTER 8

Special Situations

Special situations are situations that a company experiences that can be lucrative for penny stock investors. These situations are caused by internal and external factors. A special situation can be the development of a new drug by a pharmaceutical company that promises to eradicate AIDS. Special situations can also include penny stocks making a transition from one stock market to another market. Another category of a special situation is an opportunity that presents itself in fast paced markets. The following special situations that will be discussed are not mean to exclude all other type of situations you should look for. The chapter should help you understand what type of situations can lead towards explosive results in penny stock investing. Use this chapter to develop your own list of special situations. Then you will have your own list of situations that you can learn how to spot and take advantage of.

Penny stock companies are unique among all public securities in the sense that they live in obscurity. There are analysts working for every major Wall Street firm covering all types of securities from American depository receipts to Brazilian mining stocks. Penny stocks do not have any analysts covering their every move. They do not have the benefit of having Wall Street firms issuing opinions on them. They languish in obscurity until they have one major break through. Once they have that major break through Wall Street will start taking notice of them. It will all start with an article written on the Bloomberg news wire being picked up by

the established media outlets. Business editors at the media outlets will decide if the story warrants further attention. Providing
that the story is of national interest the company will be featured
on Bloomberg and CNBC. At that point the NY Times and Wall
Street Journal will write a short paragraph on the company. In one
month the name a company that languished in the shadows of
obscurity will be on the tip of every investor's tongue.

What kind of an event could create such a large stir for a penny
stock company?

The production of an innovative product that will change the
market place has the potential to garner national attention. Two
years ago a small brokerage firm forged ahead with online trading
before the big boys had entered the market. With day trading
becoming the focus of every media outlet, company that promised
to provide even easier and cheaper access to trading made for an
interesting article. The small brokerage firm would let investors
save over 75% what they were paying their brokers to place trades.
The traders could now place trades themselves from any computer
terminal. The name of this company was JB Oxford. The price of
its stock rose from .40 on December 98 to $24 by March 99.
Investors in JB Oxford saw their JBOH holdings increase in value
by 6000% in three months. To put it in other words, an investment of $10,000 in JB Oxford in December was worth $600,000
three months later.

The amount of profits you can generate by holding a penny
stock that receives national exposure is tremendous. Penny stocks
that have the potential to receive national publicity need to meet
at least one of the following criteria. Penny stocks meeting all of
the following criteria have an excellent chance of being the focus of
the media very soon.

The product of the company needs to have the immediate
potential to change its market. JB Oxford introduced online discount trading at a time when most investors were still conducting
their trades the old fashioned way over the phone. The product
must face little or no competition in a market with huge demand.

A company developing a product to reduce gas consumption in cars would be met with a tremendous amount of demand from every motorist tired of emptying out their wallet at the pump. The product should solve a pressing problem that does not have any other solutions. I would guarantee that if a penny stock company discovered the cure for AIDS its stock would soon trade for over $100.

The key for opening the door to the national media is based on being able to promote the company and product. In order for a company to be effectively promoted they need to hire the best Investor Relations and Public Relations firms. Publicity is an area that small business should splurge on. Without publicity they will become only another listing in the yellow book. But the right PR firm will know who to call and what to say to obtain coverage for their client in the major newspapers. Having a great product without great publicity is like having a great idea but keeping it to a secret. No matter how good the idea is no one will ever know about it. Later on we will discuss Investor and Public Relations firm.

Another great situation you should look for is the transition of your stock from the market it trades at to another market. The dream of every small company is to obtain a listing on a larger market. OTC stocks work hard on meeting listing requirements for the Nasdaq market. The penny stocks will receive more exposure to Wall Street on the Nasdaq market than they ever will on the bulletin board. Analysts will initiate coverage of them once they trade on Nasdaq. Mutual funds will now be able to buy up the stock of the former bulletin board company. Brokers at most large firms cannot recommend penny stocks to their clients. But once the stock trades on a large market the company will have the opportunity of having its stock recommended by brokers to their clients. The buying from mutual fund managers is enough to increase the market cap of the smallest Nasdaq company.

There are strict requirements for a company to be listed on the Nasdaq. The requirements pertain to stock price, revenues, and other listing requirements. Very few penny stocks will ever fulfill the requirements needed for listing on the Nasdaq. The ones that do will now be valued in an entirely different category. Your radar should be programmed to find penny stocks that are ready to make the move to Nasdaq.

Pink sheet stocks are even more ignored than over the counter stocks. Penny stocks are companies that have not filed their financials with the SEC. There is very little information on them. The lack of transparency discourages even penny stock investors from placing buy orders for pink sheet stocks. The lack of interest from investors keeps the price of pink sheet stocks down. Most of the pink sheet stocks deserve to have their price kept down because of the state of affairs at the company. The management does not return investor phone calls and acts like they are working at a private firm. It is very common to call a pink sheet stock and get a recording informing you that the number has been disconnected. Their offices are often one room suites used by another business. Then why mention them at all if they appear to be worthless? The reason you should still consider pink sheet stocks is some of them do not deserve to be on the pink sheets. They are there because the company could not afford the $100,000 it can cost to have lawyers and accountants prepare the filings. Management needs to make hard decisions when resources are tight. There are payroll obligations every month regardless of the condition of the stock. Rent needs to be paid or the company will be forced out to the streets. Priorities dictate that companies must sometimes fall back on external needs to satisfy inner needs. Once the internal needs have been satisfied companies can move on to work on their external secondary requirements.

Pink sheet companies that file their financials and are moving to be listed on the over the counter market can make great investments. Penny stock investors have ignored this stock for a long time. The company might not even have had operations in the past. Dormant companies will file when they are ready to launch their businesses because they know that they will be able to get hold of funding when they are a reporting company trading on a more liquid market. Lenders will often lend money against stock. In the event that the company defaults on its loans the lender will take an agreed upon number of shares in lieu of the loan amount. If the company stock trades on the pink sheets the lender will find it very hard to liquidate the stock. There is very little liquidity on the pink sheets. Any substantial sale of stock in the pink sheets will pummel the price down since there are no buyers on the other side. The pink sheet company realizes that once they start trading on the OTC their stock can be used as collateral for loans.

An OTC stock has other advantages. It can be used to make acquisitions of private companies that would not want to be bought by a pink sheet stock. The management of the company can also purchase other OTC companies using their stock. Once they make the transition form being a pink sheet stock to an over the counter stock the price of the stock should move up accordingly. Penny stock investors will have more respect for the management company now that its executives took the time and money to become fully reporting. Investors know that the company has spent over $100,000 to become reporting. No one would spend that amount of money unless they had solid plans through which they can later on recuperate the money spent. A business owner would only spend thousands of dollars on remodeling his place of business if he planned on being in business for the long term. Otherwise he would pocket the money and focus on more short-term usages for his money. The use of a sizable amount of money for an expense that does not add to the immediate bottom line of the company is clearly a long-term investment. Investors at this point will not buy up the stock until they see it trading on the over the counter market. The reason for their wait is to ensure that they are in fact buying an over the counter stock. Investors will be concerned that after buying the stock the company's financials will be rejected by the SEC and the company will remain a pink sheet stock. To avoid being in this situation you should call the company and find out who is working on their financials. Preferably the accounting firm doing the audit should have experience auditing public firms. The law firm that will do the actual filing should have a successful track record. The law firm's record should include having obtained listings for other public companies wishing to become listed on the OTC. The filing process is lengthy and can take months so be prepared to be patient. The wait is worth the time if you bought the stock for less than .05 and now you are sitting on what potentially could turn out to be a .25 stock. If you take a look at any 10 random fully reporting OTC stocks you will discover that most of them trade for over .10. Using that number, if you buy a pink sheet stock that is trying to become fully reporting for less than .05 you can do very well once the stock is fully reporting.

Situations worth investing in are not restricted to company events. The situations can apply to the stock of the company without being connected to the company. There are situations when investor enthusiasm builds up for stock. Day traders notice the price of the stock slowly increasing and they jump in to buy the stock. The first day traders to pounce on the stock sharply push up the price. Lake a pack of hungry wolves other day traders want to buy in before the price continues escalating. Regular investors get caught up in the frenzy and join in buying up the stock. As the buying slows the early day traders take their profits. Selling waves follow the slowing down of buying. The day traders quickly put in sell orders. They want to get out while they still can take a profit. This situation is called momentum trading. The momentum of the price movement draws in buyers and compels sellers to get out.

Momentum trading is caused when a stock is mentioned in a newsletter and investors rush in to buy the stock. Momentum traders look to make money from quick price changes. They rush to buy the stock when they receive an email on it before other investors react to the stock tip. As other investors respond to the newsletter the stock price rapidly goes up. The first few buyers will start selling the stock when the buying slows. This trading situation is very common with low priced penny stocks. An email

reaching 1000 investors covering a .05 stock will have a remark-
able effect on the price. The buyers will rush to buy up the stock.
Market makers will raise their price because they do not have much
of a supply of the stock and they see all the buying demand that
there is for the stock. Investors will see the price go up and they
will be convinced that the price is headed higher. They will also
place orders seconds apart from the last order for the stock. I have
seen stocks in this situation rise from .05 to .40 within an hour
only to crash back down to .10 as the selling starts.

The only way to profit from momentum trading is to place
your buy as soon as you receive the email. You should always use a
limit order when buying a penny stock, and especially with momentum trading since the price changes so fast. Do not fall into
the trap of chasing the price as it moves up. If you keep chasing
the price and catch it at the end of the run you will sadly regret
your purchase as the price rapidly declines. Momentum trading is
extremely risky since only the first few investors make money.
Momentum investing can be profitable if you are disciplined and
check your greed at the door. Decide exactly what price you are
willing to pay for the stock and stick to it. Immediately after receiving confirmation of having bought the stock place your next
trade. Your next trade should be a limit sell. Do not get let your
greed over take you. Many investors hold off selling the stock because they see the price going higher and higher. You need to be
one of the few disciplined investors who can place a sell order five
minutes later and walk away with a small but decent profit. Stick
to this method and all the small profits you make along the way
will add up in a short time.

CHAPTER 9

Insiders

The term Insiders is used to refer to the employees and officers of a public company. They are on the inside of a company opposed to the investors who only learn about the company through information released by those insiders. Having an inside information in a public company puts an individual in position of power. The individual can react to the information before anyone on the outside of the company can. For example, the sales manager of a life insurance company will know the exact number of policies sold in the quarter. He can use that knowledge to buy the stock or sell it before anyone has a chance to react to the information. The problem would arise when the sales manager knows that the quarter was profitable and he starts buying up the stock. The price moves up before the information becomes public. Once the news is released that the quarter was profitable investors buy the stock based on the assumption that the news is not factored in to the price. They expect the price to move up from the point that the news is released. If the price has already gone up based on the manager's buying the investors will not see the price appreciation that they expected. On the other hand, if the sales manager, his family, and who ever else he told to buy the stock, wait for the news to be released, then everyone can buy the stock without being afraid that the price already reflects the news.

Or if bad is going to be released, the CEO could start buying shares in the market to confuse investors. Investors attribute the price increase to anticipated good news. Thinking that they are taking advantage of an early sign of good news they buy the stock when it is rising. Once the news is released they realize that they have been had. The CEO could have done this to unload shares through a friend or in an attempt to keep up the price.

The SEC made it illegal to trade based on inside information to protect investors. The playing field is leveled when everyone has access to the same information. Insiders are still allowed to buy their stock or sell their stock based on public information. The issue becomes murky in determining if an insider is buying based on public information or inside information when no seeming event took place. Insiders will always be the first ones to know of a development ahead of outsiders. They rationalize their purchases of shares by claiming that they are buying based on the general outlook of the company. They will say that they are not buying based on any private piece of information. Their transactions become legal and the SEC will usually not look into them unless their trades are timed to occur within a short time of a major event.

It pays to follow the trading activity of insiders. Insiders are required to file their planned purchases and sales so you can easily see what they are doing. By following their trading activity you can determine if they are positive or negative on their company's direction. If an insider feels that his company will have an exceptionally profitable he will buy stock in his company. Although he may not be buying based on inside information he still has a much better take on the company than an outsider can. He speaks to customers on a daily basis, has meetings with the other executives, and speaks to the company accountant every Friday. The closer the individual is to the CEO the more information he will know. The CEO knows everything about the company since his role in the business is to be responsible for all aspects of the company. If you see the CEO selling stock you know that's it time to jump ship.

Everything has to be taken with a grain of salt. A CEO selling 5,000 shares of his company might not be responding to bad news within the company. He can simply be freeing up funds to buy a new car. Compare his total holdings to the number of shares he is selling. A sale of 1% of his holdings would not be considered significant enough to warrant you to sell your shares. Chances are that if the CEO believed that his company was headed for disaster he would sell allot more than 1% of his holdings. Buying by the CEO should be taken as a good sign even if he is only buying a few thousand shares. He would not buy shares if he did not feel that the stock was a good investment. No one wants to throw away good money. If you are wondering why the CEO would not buy more shares if he felt it was such a good investment call him and ask him. He will probably tell you that he has his funds tied up in other stocks at this time. He could be paying for his daughter's college tuition and that is all the money he has left. Any purchase would still be a good sign since the CEO is a human being with other financial obligations like the rest of us. He would not spend money buying his stock unless he knew that it would perform better than other stocks trading in the market.

If you are unsure as to the direction of a company based on the trading of an insider compare his trading to the trading of other insiders. If you see various filings to sell by insiders then you know that there is a consensus by the insiders that the company is headed south.

Many companies have policies that allow insiders to sell shares at set intervals. By alerting investors that insiders will be selling on a set basis panic is avoided. Investors understand that the selling is not in response to the condition of the company. The policy enables insiders to sell their shares without causing a steep decline in the price of the stock. Through this policy shareholders benefit from being provided with a reason not to be alarmed by the selling. Insiders gain by being able to sell their stock in the company. A large percentage of the compensation that management receives is based on equity so management needs an easy way to be able to cash in their stock. Without the capability to periodically sell stock the executives would not have the motivation that comes from owning an appreciating stock.

Various reasons can arise for management selling stock in a company. The executives might need to free up cash to pay their taxes. Or they might be accepting stock instead of an annual salary. Start-up companies that cannot afford to pay their employees a salary compensate their employees through the usage of stocks and stock options. The employees are counting on the value of the stocks to provide the money they will need. The employees will be motivated to make the company succeed since they know that the better the company does the more valuable their stocks become. Even if the employees are convinced that the stock is headed even higher, at some point they will need to sell the stock they are holding to pay for the mundane expenses of life.

If you want to ensure that the management of a company is concerned with the performance of the stock make sure that they own stock in the company. Just owning stock in the company is not enough to ensure that they will work hard to keep up the share price. You want to make sure that the insiders own at least 20% of the company. A 20% stake in a small company is substantial enough to ensure that they will consider the company their own. They will measure their wealth by the price of the stock if they have a major ownership position in the company. A CEO with 5,000,000 shares will act very differently than a CEO of a similarly priced stock who only owns 10,000 shares. The CEO with the 5,000,000 shares knows that if the stock rises from .20 to .50 he has just increased his net worth by $1,500,000, enough money to buy a small hotel. The CEO with only 10,000 shares is not financially impacted by the performance of the stock. A .20 move in either direction would only mean $2,000 to him, while to the other CEO it would mean $1,000,000. Imagine how the CEO with the larger stake feels when his company makes a mistake that negatively impacts the value of his shares. Wouldn't you love to have the CEO of the company directly concerned with the price of your investment?

Insiders that own a large stake in their company are making it very clear to the world that they have confidence in the direction of the stock. If they had lost confidence in the ability of the stock they would have reduced their ownership to lower levels. The insiders know that they cannot sell large amounts of their shares at once or the stock price would plummet. This means that if they want to sell their holdings they only have two options. They can either sell small amounts of stock every month, or they can wait for the price to be high enough that even if the price starts decreasing as they sell the price will still be high enough for them to make money. So if you see that insiders are not slowly reducing their ownership stake they must be holding the stock counting on future appreciation.

The 20% figure is not a black and white rule. Insiders might have had to give up 90% of the company to venture capitalists. Venture capitalists fund companies before they are public in exchange for a major stake in the company.

At the same time you would not want to buy the stock of a company in which the insiders reduced their stake by a major percentage. A company in which the insiders own 30% of the company should be treated very carefully if the insiders had owned 50% of the company the prior month. You need to question why the insiders felt the need to reduce their equity position. The reason can be as simple as some of the positive reasons we discussed before, or the reason for the sale can have to do with a management that lacks faith in its company.

It is very challenging for the average investor to comprehend the true state of the company's affairs. Management will not send us a copy of their business plan. The investor relations firm will try to paint a rosy picture of any company development. I once had an investor relations' spokesperson for a penny stock explain to me why his company would benefit from being de listed. Another investor relations' person was trying to educate me on how shareholders had benefited from a "short term" 50% drop in the price of their stock. While most investor relation firms are highly professional and factual some of them will say anything to get you to buy the stock. Then how do you know the true condition of a company?

Follow the positions of institutional investors. Institutional investors are money management firms, insurance firms, mutual funds, money managers, investment banks and other financial firms. By following their investment decisions you will know if they approve of a stock as good investment. The problem with that is you cannot follow the investment decisions of investment firms that are private entities. Then why did I make a suggestion that is impractical at best?

Because the answer is that you can follow the investment decisions of those firms. You might not be able to see which stocks they hold in their portfolios, but you can see which stocks institutional investors own. How?

There are financial web sites that provide information as to how many institutions own a stock and what percentage of the outstanding stock is owned by institutional investors. This information is highly valuable because of the nature of an institutional investor. An institutional investor manages money for individuals or for its own benefit. The people who have given money to institutions to be managed expect and demand a high level of diligence. People will not give money to an institution that repeatedly loses money, especially when the loss could have been avoided through thorough research of the investment. Institutional investors face the added pressure of having to work in a very competitive market. There are thousands of brokers, money managers, hedge fund managers, and mutual fund managers competing for the right to manage money. The competitiveness of the money management business is augmented by the fact that people measure results by the bottom line. A fund manager with a 30% loss in a bull market will not attract any business regardless of how nice of an individual he is. The investment bank that delivers profitable equity private placements to its clients earns the right to delay returning phone calls, something that if done in any other industry would repel clients.

Faced with the intense competition of having to produce profits and maximize investor returns while guarding against risk, they need to be very careful when choosing their investments. This leads them to doing an immense amount of research before investing their money in any company. This does not mean that they stay away from penny stocks. An entire section of the financial industry specializes in micro cap companies. Penny stocks to those who do their research and can tolerate the risk offer some of the best returns in the market. Institutional investors realize this and participate in this market.

Your job is to make sure that the penny stock you are considering has institutional ownership. A stock that is owned by an institutional investor has been thoroughly researched by the firm's analysts. Analysts visit the corporate headquarters and pour over the financials with the treasurer. They spend an extensive amount of time studying the market that the company operates in. Interviews are conducted with employees at all levels of the company. Only after receiving a positive rating from their analysts will an institutional investor buy stock in the company.

They are offered stock at below the market price to encourage them to buy stock in the company. The motivation for the company to sell their stock at a discount is that they need operating funds for their business. The process starts with the company experiencing a need for money. Using an investment bank to solicit funds from institutions they start contacting large investors. The job of the investment bank is to find an institution that would be willing to buy enough shares to meet the financial needs of the company.

After researching the company they are considering investing in the institutional investor will make an offer. The offer will be a request for a certain amount of stock in exchange for the funds that they will give the company. The penny stock company can either agree or update their offer for the funds from the large investor. After much haggling the institutional investor will buy the stock for 20% to 50% below the market price of the stock. The stock will be restricted for at least a year adding to the risk that the institutional investor is taking. To compensate for this risk the investment entity will require that it buy the stock for a discount to its current trading price. This way if the price drops the investment group is still protected up to a degree. And if the stock does as well as planned the investment will be worth that much more than if it was simply bought on the open market. Proceeds from stocks bought on the open market do not go to the company. The only way for the company to receive funds from investors is to sell them stock directly.

At this point the institutional investor will own shares in the company and will closely monitor the progress of the company. Because of the money it has at stake it might even provide advice and counsel to help the company succeed. Restrictions on the stock make it a long-term investment. As a result the institutional investor will do what it can to ensure that the price of the stock heads higher from buying up stock in the open market to assisting in the management of the company. The investment entity can be the average investor's finest ally. Their money is tied up in the same place as yours is. For this reason you would want the added security of owning a penny stock with institutional ownership.

While a penny stock with institutional ownership has received a sort of stamp of approval the opposite is not necessarily true. Just because a penny stock does not have institutional shareholders does not mean that it is a bad stock to invest in. The penny stock you are looking at could have taken a different approach to solicit funds. It could have avoided having to look for money if its founders invested their own money in the company. In that case I think it is safe that the founders really believe in the long-term success of their company.

The penny stock company could have generated enough cash through its business to fund all operations. Many penny stocks were once private firms that have gone public after they existed as a profitable business for many years.

The penny stock you are looking at could have obtained funds from wealthy investors through a private placement. In a private placement the company meets with certified investors and negotiates the sale of stock at favorable terms in exchange for cash.

Once the company has obtained the funds it requires it will not approach institutional investors unless it needs at a later point.

Institutional shareholders in a penny stock should be treated as an extra bonus. You know that they have researched and met extensively with the company before investing their money in the stock. A penny stock investor that wants to play it more conservatively, might want to restrict his penny stock investing to companies with institutional investors. Keep in mind that unless you know the institution you could be making a big mistake assuming that they are a credible entity. Call up the institution the same way you would call up a company you are considering investing in.

Warning, there are many tricks that can be played by institutions to the detriment of the average investor. There have been reports of entities shorting a stock they have invested in. As soon as the shares they have bought become unrestricted they dump them on the market. They establish a small profit from the shares they have dumped on the market. The real profit they make is made from covering their short positions after the price of the penny stock collapses. The price collapses as a result of all the selling done by the entity and the selling triggered by panicked investors who sell after seeing the huge sells from the entity. As the price settles at a much lower level than where it started at the entity buys back stock at a much lower price. They use that stock that they have bought at a much lower price to return it to the brokers they borrowed the stock from when they shorted it.

Find out when the stock held by institutional investors becomes free trading. Even if they have no nefarious intentions they will sell shares when they become free trading. It is understandable since they have been holding their shares for a while now and they must show their investors a return on their money. They will sell at small increments to avoid the stock from collapsing, as long as they are not involved in any short selling activity. Ninety nine percent of institutional investors are ethical and rely on legitimate trading techniques. There is enough of a profit that can be made by institutions investing in micro caps to avoid having to resort to shady business.

No reputable firm would involve itself in any transaction that appears to involve fraud. The last thing they need is an investigative article published about them in a leading newspaper. Bad publicity will only persuade investors to grab their money and run for the door. The long-term players in the money management business know that it takes years to build up a reputation and only a day to ruin it.

CHAPTER 10

Research

Research is the cornerstone for success in penny stock investing. Without learning how to research you will have to resort to following other people's advice. You will be in the position of having to be a follower waiting for investment advice from newsletters and web sites. Rather than be a follower led by those who know how to perform research become a leader. Leaders do not have all the answers but know how to obtain them. They use their intuition developed from accumulated experience to make sound assessments. You can become a leader among the masses of penny stock investors by learning to refine your research skills. I am certain beyond a doubt that you have the ability to develop great research skills. I know that you already have decent research skills based on the fact that you have found this book and decided to read it. You can expand those skills if you are willing to put in the effort and time. This chapter will teach you how to expand your research methods to discover the most promising penny stock investments.

Determining the size of the company is an important step in establishing the actual condition of the company. A company with many employees needs to meet a much higher payroll than a company with a few employees. The cost of the payroll is an expense that is recurrent and must be paid as frequently as twice a month. There is now way to get around this expense outside of paying the employees with stock. Companies can at the beginning compensate their employees with stock but at some point he employees will need to receive a standard paycheck. As the company grows and hires level entry positions they will be forced to pay them with a regular paycheck. A level entry-level employee with a family to support will be unable to accept stock instead of a regular paycheck. What this means to us is that if we see that the penny stock company has many employees it must be making enough money to pay the employees. The more employees the company employs the more revenues it is generating or the more cash it has on hand to pay them. Having many employees also tells us that they are engaged in a real business that requires hard work from many employees. This message also tells us that they are not a boiler room operation or a company simply looking to push up its stock price and dump their shares unto the market. By hiring many employees the company is making a long-term commitment to its business.

Now that we have established the reason why having many employees is a positive sign we need to find out how to determine the number of employees. One way to go about finding out the number of employees is to look up the company profile on a financial web site. If the information is not provided you should up the human resources manager for the company and ask her the number. Introduce yourself to her and let her know why you want to know the information. By being honest with her she will be at ease and friendly towards you. If you have any trouble finding out this number call the CEO and let him know that you are a shareholder in his company and would like to receive the number according to disclosure rules for publicly traded companies.

When you speak to the human resources human manager ask her if she is hiring. Find out what positions she is looking people and the requirements for the positions. A company that is hiring employees is looking to grow and expand. The company must be doing well if they want to hire additional employees. A company that is hiring has the funds to pay employees salaries, and is expecting future income to cover the ongoing salaries of the employees.

A company reducing its work force is facing difficulties of a financial or business nature. Management has decided that they will not have the necessary revenue to pay those employees salaries so they fire them. The difficulty could be an expected or future financial loss, or the loss of a source of revenue. A company that has lost a major contract will fire the employees that it used to service the contract. Executives from the company will try to put a positive spin on the workforce reduction so you need to carefully read between the lines.

If the human resources manager tells you that they are hiring employees it is very important to find out for what positions and what requirements the applicants need to have. For one thing, you might be able to help them and someone you know by matching them up with the company. From a research standpoint the information is invaluable. The positions that the company is looking to fill will tell you everything you need to know about the direction of the company.

A human resources manager for a book publisher looking for a web site developer with e commerce experience should tell you allot. The book publisher must be planning on developing a web site through which they plan on selling books. Why else would they hire a web site developer with e commerce experience?

The CEO or investor relations department would never let you know this information ahead of time but you can find it out for by yourself. Call the human resources manager and discuss with her the exact requirements and needs of the company for the position they are looking to fill.

I remember reading a display advertisement in the Wall Street Journal job section for an e commerce specialist position at a regional bank. I knew at that point after reading the advertisement that the bank was planning on starting an Internet banking operation. Soon enough, the company announced that they would be offering banking services over the Internet to their clients. The stock of the bank rose 20% on the news. Imagine if you had seen the advertisement and bought the stock a week before anyone else the news. You could have made a 20% return in a one week period based on a single piece of information you could have also obtained from the human resources manager of the company. Make it a habit to call the human resources manager or the person with the responsibility of hiring at the penny stocks you are considering investing in.

A company is comprised of many interlocking departments that depend on each other to perform their roles in the company. The marketing department prepares materials for the sales department that brings in clients for the account executives to work with. The health of the company is strongly influenced by the ability of these departments to carry out their respective roles and interact with each other. A company with a marketing department that has a deep understanding of the company's product will know how to promote the product effectively. They will understand the need that the product fills and the customers who are most likely to respond to the benefits offered by the product. The same goes for the sales department and the corporate suite. Every department is an essential component of the company.

Call each department and spend time talking to them. Pose as a customer and make product inquiries. Determine if the sales department is enthusiastic about their product. Were they able to answer all your questions to your satisfaction? Could they have sold you on the product if you were in the market for it? Did the receptionist answer your calls promptly? Did the various departments return your phone calls in a timely fashion? Remember, the way they treated you is the way they will treat potential customers and business associates. If they lacked in professionalism and enthusiasm they will not last in business.

Call the suppliers of the company. This information can be next to impossible to obtain but if you are successful in obtaining it you will know allot more than the average investor will ever know. You can try to ask the CEO if he considers his suppliers reliable to supply him with the resources he needs to conduct business on a long-term basis. Proceed by discussing his answer and slowly collecting as much implied and direct information he gives you regarding his suppliers. He might say that his supplier has been in business for over 25 years and is a member of the Better Business Bureau. Try to find out which city his supplier is located in. You can then call the BBB directly and ask for a list of paper suppliers that are members of the Bureau in that city. Call each one and tell them that you are considering doing business with the company, make sure that the business you mention is unrelated so they know that you are not trying to steal their customer. When you find the supplier that does business with the penny stock company ask them how about their relationship.

Your aim is to find out if the company pays its bills on time and if it is in good standing with its suppliers. If the supplier warns you that the company does not pay their bills on time you can make the assumption that the company is not doing as well as it seems. If the supplier lets you know that he will soon be dropping them as a customer you know that the company is in trouble.

The CEO might be forthcoming with information if you are above board with him and explain to him why you want to speak to his suppliers. Tell him that as part of your research you prefer to speak to outside parties that interact with the company.

Another way to discover the identity of a supplier is by ordering a product from the penny stock company. When you receive the product you can examine it and try to determine who makes the various parts that make up the unit.

Your goal is to find out how suppliers view the company. They also conduct research on the company to ensure that the client will be a paying customer and will not cause them trouble. Suppliers can request a credit report on the company as part of their initial research into the company. The supplier also requests the phone number of the company's banker so he can make sure that the company has the funds to pay for their orders. In short, once a supplier has accepted a company as a customer you know that the company must be in good standing with its supplier. Meaning it pays its bills in a timely manner and can meet its financial obligations.

Customers are a great source of information. Customers are users of the product or service of the penny stock company.

They are very easy to find. You can call the CEO and tell him you
would like to speak to some of his customers for research purposes
or you can pose again as a potential customer and ask for references
from the sales department. The sales department will want to gain
your confidence as a prospective customer. The sales department
knows that to establish a customer relationship with a new person
they will need to supply the names of other customers who have
used their service. Of course, they will only give you the names
and phone numbers of people who love their product. Some companies might even pay people to pose as satisfied customers. You
can tell the actors from the real customers apart by asking diligent
questions about the product that only a true user would know the
answers to. You can ask them if the product holds up in specific
conditions and what the result of using it over an extended period
of time is. The real customers will not have that much time to
discuss the product with you since they have other business to
attend to. They will give you direct and honest answers. The paid
references will spend allot of time on the phone with you selling
the product. The real customers will inquire about you and your
use for the product out of curiosity as to whom they are talking to.
The paid reference does not care, he knows his job is to extol the
virtues and will not care who you are or how you even got his
number.

Once you are sure that you are speaking to a genuine customer find out how long he has used the product or service. Ask
him if he is satisfied with the product, what the benefits and det-
riments of the product are. Find out if he is satisfied with the
service he receives from the company. Do they communicate on a
timely basis? Are they helpful with information on the product?

Companies that go out of their way to service customers will
gain many more customers through word of mouth. They will
grow as they gain more customers who are referred to them by
their current customers. Customers are the lifeblood of any business; those who have strong customer relationships will always
have a steady supply of blood flowing to their heart. Those who do

not take extra care of their customers will soon find that they do not have any customers to service.

There is competition in any business. The obvious type of competition is the one between two restaurant chains competing for customers in a metropolitan area. You will find many penny stocks that are involved in the restaurant business. Be warned, that the restaurant business has the highest rate of failure among all businesses.

Less obvious sources of competition are two companies offering vacation packages. One company might offer a cruise to Alaska, while the other one might offer a 5-ight stay at a hotel in Arizona. At first glance they do not seem to be competing. The vacation packages are located in different locations and are quite different in details. But they are both in direct competition when you realize that people can only take limited vacations every year and must decide what they prefer doing on what very often is there only vacation for the year. The cruise operator and hotel are both in the vacation business and their potential customer is the family planning its annual vacation.

You need to determine who the competition is for the penny stock you are considering investing in. After coming up with a short list of competitors for your penny stock you need to work the phone. Call each one of them and discuss the general market with them. You want to know if the market is big enough to support many entrants into the field. Is there enough business for everyone or is a winner take all market? Are they familiar with the company you are considering investing in? They will usually be frank and tell you what they think of the company.

Your goal is to learn about the market the penny stock is operating in and the opportunity to make money in it. If the competitors are entrenched in the field the penny stock will have a very hard time surviving in the field. On the other hand if you call the competitors and they turn out to be inept or incompetent in serving the market you know that the penny stock has a very good chance at capturing the market.

Trade organizations are a good source for information on a penny stock and on the market the penny stock operates in. Companies join trade organizations to receive the benefits of belonging to an organization. The organization can use its collective purchasing ability to work out deals with vendors for its members. A trade organization consisting of Internet providers can obtain cheaper health insurance rates for its members by using all its members to bargain. By offering the health insurer a large number of customers it will be able to secure a discount that a small single company could not. Trade organizations also lobby lawmakers on behalf of their members when they are faced with legal issues that will affect them.

Memberships in trade organizations are usually restricted to members who meet strict criteria. Trade organizations do not want to tarnish their images by having members who are involved in illegal or questionable business practices. When you see a business listed in a trade organization you know that the business must be meeting the requirements of its membership and not violating any principles that would exclude it from the organization. The rules and principles for membership in trade organizations are available to the public.

Ask the investor relations contact person for the penny stock for a list of trade organizations the company is a member of. You want to make sure that the company is a member of the Better Business Bureau, Chamber of Commerce, and a relevant trade organization. By being a member of these organizations you will be a step closer to knowing that the penny stock is not a boiler room operation but a real business with real operations. Next, you want to contact the trade organizations and ask them for how long they have been members. You also want to know if they have received any complaints regarding the company. If they have not received any complaints and they have been members for over 3 years you know at least that the company is not changing its name every time complaints are made and that the company is in good standing since it has no complaints against it.

Discuss the penny stock with the person you speak to at the trade organization. The conversation will provide you with additional information you might not have known. The representative you speak to will be able to tell you what he knows about them. Compare the information he or she tells you with the information that the company gives you. By comparing the information that you have been given you will be able to ascertain if the penny stock represented itself to you factually.

Trade organizations will provide you with an accurate description of the market their members participate in. They will provide you with information such as the seasonal lows and peaks for the business cycle. You would prefer to buy stock in a penny stock when the market it is operating in is at its low so you can reap the profits from the stock when the penny stock makes its way back during its peak cycle. To put it more bluntly, you want to buy an ice cream wholesaler during the winter season when sales are low and its stock is low and sell it when the summer season brings sales and the stock back up. The trade organizations will tell you when the up and down periods are for the business.

Trade organizations can also tell you what the success rate is for new entrants to the market. They might tell you that only 10% of new entrants last a second year in the market. If this is the case you better make sure that your penny stock has what it takes to be that 10%.

Trade organizations will supply you with literature concerning all aspects of the market. Information will include the market size, number of companies operating in the market, average profits for the companies, and other assorted information pertaining to their members. The information can tell you what the penny stock can expect if it succeeds in the market that it operates. Assuming that no company can capture more than 5% of its market, you should realize that at best the penny stock would only have sales equaling 5% of the total market size. A market worth $10,000,000 would only provide $500,000 of sales to the average successful company. A market worth $500,000,000 would be worth

$25,000,000 to the micro cap that captures 5% of it. Using this information you would be correct if you decided to only concentrate on penny stocks operating in markets worth over $100,000,000. I have heard many companies promise that they will capture 80% of the market within 5 years. The problem is that every company in the same field has the same goals, and once customers are satisfied with one vendor they usually stay with them for life.

Trade organizations are your window into a field you might lack knowledge in. If you decide to specialize in one filed in your penny stock investing you should find all the trade organizations that represent the players in the field. You might even be able to find out from them who the rising star in their field is. Once you know that a small company is taking the market by storm you only have to buy its stock and sit back while the price increases. To find out this information you will have to develop relationships with people at the trade organizations. Keep their business cards in your Rolodex and write down their numbers in your business phone book. Call them up once a month to find out if there are any new developments in the field. All you need is one call to point you in the right direction and you might find the next penny stock that will someday be listed on the Nasdaq.

Speak to the CEO of the penny stock you are looking at. This advice might seem obvious but you would be surprised how many investors are satisfied with only speaking to the investor relations department. The investor relations department specializes in speaking to investors. They will be helpful but they will also measure their words down to the inch. The CEO will be more willing to discuss his business with you especially if he is the founder of the company. You will need to call him up and request a time when you can call him back and discuss the company in depth with him. His first reaction will be to refer you to the investor relations department. Tell him that you have already spoken to them and that you would really enjoy speaking to him to learn more about the business. If he completely refuses then you know that there probably is nothing much to talk about. The phrase "fly by night operation" should start creeping into your head at this point. Chief executive officers know the importance of investors to a small company. The CEOs of legitimate companies will set up a time to talk to you. They will be brief due to their heavy workload so you must be prepared with a list of questions and be focused on the aspects of the company you are interested in.

You should develop a relationship with the CEO by her periodically and complementing her on positive steps the company has taken. The more you show an interest in the company the more the CEO will be inclined to share information with you. As time goes by she will see you as a loyal investor and will seek to find ways to reward you for your support and interest in the stock. She could invite you to a conference the company will be participating in. You might be invited to visit the company and given a tour of the company. Having a relationship with the CEO or other top officer at a company is the optimum approach for getting information on the company.

Creditors are useful sources for determining the financial strength of the company. Creditors are entities to which money is owed to by the company. They have become creditors by extending credit to the company for the sales of products or services. There is a 30-day time period for business buyers to pay their bills similar to the grace period provided by your credit card company for you to pay your bill. The 30-day period is considered credit that has been extended to the customer. Your penny stock is has received credit form most of the entities it makes purchases from.

By contacting creditors you can find out how much money the penny stock owes and the time they have left to pay it back. A penny stock that has defaulted on its credit will face a collection department. If the debt is not resolved creditors will call in the money they are owed and will no longer extend credit to the company. A lack of credit makes it very difficult if not impossible for a company to operate. The company will not receive payment for its output for 30 days. If it has to pay for its goods at the beginning of

the month and then wait another 30-60 days for payment on the
goods it has sold the company will face a severe cash shortage. If
your penny stock is in the situation where it does not receive credit
make sure that it has enough cash to hold it over until it receives
payment from its customers. If you find out that creditors refuse
to extend credit to the penny stock while they are extending credit
to other companies in the market you know that the penny stock
is probably in serious danger of entering bankruptcy protection.
This is because creditors are not able to collect money that is owed
to them by a firm in bankruptcy protection, so they will not extend credit to a company that is close to entering bankruptcy protection. Suppliers have the experience to be able to tell which company is on the road to failure, therefore you should always keep
track of the actions of the creditors of the company.

The best way to keep up with the changes of the market your
penny stock is operating in is by reading. You should be reading
the magazines and trade journals covering the industry. The magazines and journals will have feature articles on developments shap-
ing the industry. The advertisements will tell you allot about the
industry. By seeing which products are being advertised and at
which prices you can measure the demand for the product that
the penny stock is offering. A multitude of advertisers for the same
product would represent a crowded market. While advertisements
dominated by a few expensive advertisers would mean that there is
room for a new entrant to the market than can offer the product at
a cheaper price.

Magazines will feature companies that are making innovative
changes in the market. Companies are being featured because they
have plenty of potential. The editors and reporters have already
investigated the companies for you and have decided that the companies have a strong product or service. In addition, the article will
create publicity for the featured company. Investors and customers will notice the company and be drawn to it. A positive article
provides more publicity than any advertisement in the same publication could. Investors will want to invest in a public company

that has received the implicit approval of the editors of a prestigious magazine. By investing in companies that have been featured in trade magazines you stand to capitalize on their continued publicity.

One of your priorities when researching a company should be to visit it. Only by visiting the company will you be able to see what is actually taking place behind close doors. A few years ago one of the largest mining frauds occurred. Investors bought up the stock of a company that claimed to have discovered an immense gold mine. Investors, including some of the largest financial institutions in the country, relied upon the opinion of others who had visited the site. They bought up the stock as it sore from under a dollar to over $70 a share before collapsing after the truth came out. The mine was a hoax. Experts had been paid off. The aftermath resulted in the stock losing its value and becoming worthless. Later on people realized that if the financial institutions had sent their own experts they would have quickly discovered that there was no gold. Billions of losses could have been spared if people had gone to visit the mine and not relied on someone else's advice.

By visiting the company you will know if the company is really engaged in the business that it claims to be in. When you are at the company look for signs of wear in the equipment and furniture. If the equipment and furniture look new after 6 months you know that no one is using them. Make sure to visit the company on a regular business day so you can see and listen to the activity of the company. The place should not be empty on a busy day. Spend time talking to the employees and offer to take one of them out to lunch to discuss the company. You will need to make the offer discretely so as not to put the employee on the spot. You do not want him to have to come under the wrath of his employer for spending his lunch hour divulging company information that management considers private.

It is crucial to ask to visit a company even if you cannot. Their answer to your request should provide you with enough information to see if they are hiding something or not. A flat out refusal to let you see the company should set off every alarm on your body. A delay in allowing you to visit the company should start the alarms unless they have a legitimate reason such as moving or remodeling the company. In that case I would postpone investing in the company until they allowed me to visit the company. Count on the fact that they might say yes assuming that you will never visit them and that you are just testing them. If they say yes, proceed with making an exact time and date to visit them. Ask them for directions from a nearby hotel. At this point they will see that you are serious about visiting them. They will either welcome you and provide directions or give you an excuse as to why this month is not good for them. You should have you answer at this point if they are a real company or just a set of temporary offices.

There is no such a thing as a policy prohibiting outside people from visiting their company. If they are afraid of corporate espionage, which is a big problem, they can meet you at the lunchroom and limit your tour to the conference room. They need to have somewhere to meet with their customers if they are a real company. Remind them of this if they refuse to let you come tour their facilities. A fly by night operation will soon hang up the phone on you if you persist. In that case do the investment community a favor and direct your next call to the SEC.

SEC fillings are the financial reports public companies are required to file. The reports consist of quarterly and annual reports. The reports will have a basic description of the company and its operations, along with financial information. Companies are very careful not to write down anything that cannot be substantiated. The SEC will come down very hard on company that fabricates its filings. Frankness is the key word when describing a quarterly report. Many companies will use the report to tell investors that they have no ongoing operations. You can read about companies whose accountants doubt that they will remain a going concern.

The SEC filings can be obtained from Edgar online, from the SEC, or from the companies. Companies will usually direct you towards a web site through which you can read their reports.

Many companies run into legal problems they work hard at hiding from the eyes of the investment community. Unfortunately for them, and fortunately for us, all legal proceedings in this country are public unless sealed by a judge. This means that you can search legal records to discover if the company has been involved in any legal proceedings. Legal proceedings should also be mentioned in the reports filed with the SEC. To get the details on the legal proceedings you can do a search using legal web sites or by examining public records. Using a legal research site enter the name of the company, the names of the top directors, shareholders, and employees and see what comes up. Once you discover legal proceedings you should ask a lawyer who you are friendly with to explain to you your findings. The legal proceeding might be uneventful. The lawsuit could be from a contractor that did not receive payment for what the company considers a poorly performed job. As long as the possible judgment against the company is small you should not be concerned with it. If the lawsuit is from a group of shareholders alleging fraud then you definitely should be extra careful in studying their allegations. Are they upset that their investment did not do well, or are they upset at being misled concerning the nature of the business the company was engaged in? A lawsuit on its own is not a reason to avoid the stock. The reason for the lawsuit is the determining factor.

Stock tip newsletters are not a good source for research. Stock tip newsletters are in essence advertisements for stocks. Most newsletters receive compensation for featuring the stock. The payment they receive is usually in the form of stock given to them by a third party. An investor with 500,000 shares of a penny stock will give the newsletter 10,000 shares for featuring the stock. The investor is planning to sell his shares when the newsletter features the stock. As buyers rush in to buy the stock that has been featured by the newsletter the investor will liquidate his position. The newsletter will provide the buyers for the stock he wants to sell by causing excitement over the stock. Without the buyers brought in by the newsletter there would not be enough demand for the stock.

The investor would see the price drop as he tried to liquidate his position. This way the price might even go up first if the investor waits to start selling his stock after an hour of buying.

The investors who bought the stock are left holding a penny stock that now has started going down as the investor dumps his shares. They assume that the newsletter was sincere and that the stock really is a good investment. They end up holding the stock until they are convinced that the price is only heading down. Their selling crushes the price of the stock.

There are stock tip newsletters that are not compensated for promoting a stock. They have disclaimers at the bottom of the page mentioning that they have not been paid by anyone to send out a newsletter or email about the stock. Then why do they send out the picks?

The answer is in the rest of the legal disclaimer. They state that they have the right to buy and sell the stock at any time without having to notify anyone of the transaction. They also may hold shares of the penny stock they are featuring. In essence what they are doing is buying up shares of a cheap penny stock and then sending out an email on it. When the price goes up they sell out earning a sizable profit in the process.

Chat rooms are a very tricky place to collect information. Chat rooms are places where investors can talk in real time with each other. They discuss stocks, market conditions, economics, and recent events. Chat rooms are dangerous places to collect information since there are many people that use them to promote the stocks that they are holding. Once excitement is created for the stock they sell out as the price rises, similarly to the way newsletters push stocks.

Chat rooms can be beneficial to penny stock investors who want to become exposed to new stocks. You will hear the name of many stocks that you can now investigate on your own. Chat rooms are also useful for asking fellow investors questions concerning finding the best broker to use, or for finding generic investment information. Never use a chat room to determine if the stock is a good investment.

Message boards are useful since they focus on one stock at a time. You will still encounter the problem of investors overtly optimistic about their stock. Investors who are overtly excited about their stock will make wild predictions that are unfounded. There will also be many investors posting negative, and sometimes false information about the stock. Their aim is to push the price down for various reasons. They could be shorting the stock through a Canadian or offshore account. They want to push down the price so they can but the stock back later for less. Or the might try to cause investors to sell the stock so the price goes down for the short term. Once the price goes down they can but the stock for a cheaper price and watch it rise in price as the fundamentals kick in. Message boards are helpful in the sense that allot of information about the company surfaces. You can then decide what to make of the information. I would suggest that information you read on the message board should be verified by calling the company directly.

All the research ideas that have been provided this far apply once you have found a penny stock you would like to invest in. But what if you have not selected a penny stock yet, how you find one to invest in?

After reading the last 100 pages you are now sure that you are ready to invest in penny stocks. You are excited at the prospect of finding the next winner and sit down at your computer ready to start your research. You start looking at the web sites recommended in this book offering pages and pages of research. You soon feel overwhelmed by all the different penny stocks being talked about and are ready to give up in frustration. You wish to yourself that there should be some way to sift through all the information to find the penny stock you are looking for.

There is an easy way to find penny stocks meeting your selection criteria. You can find penny stocks meeting your criteria through a simple news service called Business Wire. Business Wire is a news service that collects press releases from public and private companies and sends them out on its business wire.

News publications can then decided which articles they want to use in their business sections. How does this news service help you?

Business Wire updates its database as it receives press releases from companies. You can log on every day to the Business Wire web site, Businesswire.com, and read all the press releases that have been issued that day. If you do this you will find hundreds of new articles every day, sifting through all of them would be terribly time consuming and unproductive. You need to refine your search to find the articles that you want.

The Business Wire web site allows you to search for articles using key words. Since you are interested in finding press releases issued by penny stocks you need to enter a key word used by penny stock companies. Since most penny stocks are listed on the OTC market your key word will be OTC. You will then see a list of a hundred or so press releases from OTC companies. You can then scan the headlines for the articles and see if you find one that interests you.

You can take another route. Let us say that you are interested in penny stocks in the Internet field. You would then use the key words OTC and Internet in your search. Scan the articles again and pick the one out that you like.

You can do the same search using the word pink sheets for pink sheet stocks. The more key words you use the more limited your search will be. In order to refine your search make sure that you have the correct spelling for the words you are using and that you are using the correct word used by the industry. You could use the key words "penny stock" and all you would get is a list of companies that earned a penny per share.

It will take a few days of trial and error to learn how to sue the news search capabilities correctly. If you are an AOL user their news search feature can access multiple news services besides Business Wire. I use the AOL news search feature to find penny stock companies that I am interested in. I start out every morning by logging on to AOL and doing a news search. I input the word OTC and scan all the headlines that appear for that day. I read the articles that interest me and select the most promising stock based on those press releases. I then use the name of the stock as my next key word and do a search for all articles mentioning that stock. I then have a more extensive grasp on the company. If I am still interested I look up the pre market quote at Freerealtime.com and check the charts for the stock's past performance. I read the message boards by 9:20, call the company at 9:30, and by 10:00 I decide if I will buy the stock. If you are first starting out you want to spend at least a few days reading the message boards, talking to the company, and doing assorted research on the stock and company. As your experience builds you will develop an intuition to help you make decision within an hour of reading the press release and having briskly researched the company.

Make it a habit to read the press releases every morning before the market opens. If you do not have the time to read the press releases in the morning you will need to set up a time in the evening when you can go over the day's press releases. You will miss the initial price reaction after the press release was issued but you should be able to capture the long-term performance of the stock.

I recommend that you use the following key words when researching a stock. Reverse merger, Internet, profit, OTC, pink sheets, listing, featured, recommended. Make a list of your own key words. Base your key words on hot areas, sectors, products you understand, people, or even places. Oil stocks have been rising along with gas prices in the last few weeks. If the trend continues gas prices could soon be over $2 a gallon. Oil stocks are sure to follow the performance of the price of oil. You can do a search for oil penny stocks. Your two key words would be oil and OTC.

A reverse merger is the process of a public company acquiring a private company. The private company then becomes the owner of the public company and in effect is now publicly traded. The name of the public company is changed to the name of the private company and the CEO of the private firm is now the CEO of the public company. The private company has in effect merged with the penny stock and taken it over. The penny stock was only a shell prior to having been used for the merger. The penny stock did not have any operations and only existed to be used by a private company that wanted to go public without having to go through an IPO. The shareholders of the penny stock now own stock in the private business.

E Pawn used a shell to go public without having to go through an IPO. The stock of the shell traded at .09 prior to being used for the merger. After the merger people realized that the new company had value and would be worth a great deal of money if its e commerce operations were successful. The new company, which traded using the stock it was acquired with, shot up from .09 to over $8 within 4 months.

A Canadian telecommunications company earning $2,000,000 a year wanted to go public. It contacted the owner of a shell who was willing to give them a majority of the stock in exchange for owning a small remaining stake in the company after the merger took place. The telecommunications company agreed to proposal, they were bought by the public shell, which traded at .15. After the merger was finalized the company sent out an announcement that the private company would now appoint its CEO as the CEO of the public company and change its name. People realized that this worthless penny stock now owned a company earning $2 million a year. The stock had less than 4 million shares outstanding, meaning that the company would now earn .50 a share. The stock shot up in less than two weeks to $150 a share. A few lucky investors made 100 times their money in two weeks. The ticker symbol of the company is UTOU.

By this point you can understand why I am such a big fan of looking for reverse mergers. Most times reverse mergers will not come with clear labels. You will read that a company is acquiring a private company for a combination of stock and cash. You need to call the company to see if the private company will be in control. If they will only be a subsidiary then it is not a reverse merger. If they will be the only operating business for the public company then people will judge the penny stock by the performance of the private company. So although it would not literally be a reverse merger it can still have the same effect on the share price.

Avoid stocks that issue press releases with the phrase reverse split. A reverse split is an attempt to bring up the price of the stock. The company conducts a transaction in which it sends out new shares replacing a set amount of existing shares. A 10 for 1 reverse split would mean that the company would issue 1 share for every 10 shares that an investor holds. The logic is that once there are only a 10th of the shares outstanding the price would increase by 10 times. Ten old .30 shares would now be converted into one new share worth $3.00. The logic seems to work out but the problem is that investors do not feel believe that the stock can maintain its $3 price for long. After all, they remember this stock being a penny stock, not a $3 stock. Like clockwork, the stock's that have gone through reverse splits steadily drop in price until they trade at almost what they traded for prior to the split.

Companies know that this will happen but they progress non-the less. The company knows that they can only issue a certain amount of shares based on their charter. A company that has authorized 10,000,000 shares and has 5,000,000 shares outstanding can only issue another 5,000,000 shares into the market. But what if the company was presented with an opportunity that would require 6,000,000 shares to be issued to capitalize on it?

The company would do a 10 for 1 reverse split so that there would only be 500,000 shares outstanding after the split. The company is still authorized to issue 10,000,000 shares. Now that there are only 500,000 shares outstanding it can issue an additional 9 and half million shares. Before it could only issue another 5 million since it had 5 million shares outstanding. The company does not care that the price is substantially lower since it has more shares to issue to make up for the loss in price.

Investors end up losing a majority of their money after a reverse split. When I first started investing in penny stocks I bought a stock that shortly announced a reverse split. I misunderstood the details of the reverse split. I was not familiar with the concept of a reverse split and I assumed that I would simply own the same percentage of the company but under a different number of shares. I did not realize that the company would issue more shares. Two weeks after the reverse split I had lost 75% of my investment in the stock.

Press releases consist of a headline announcing a company development. The press release has the name of the company, ticker symbol, market traded on, and the location of the company under the headline. The next part of the release is the body of the PR describing the event followed by contact information for the company. There should be a name of an individual you can call at the company to ask questions regarding the PR. Depending on the company they will have both the phone number of a company employee or the phone number of their Investor Relations agency.

As part of your research into the company you want to find out how the company plans on raising funds. Every growing business at some point will need additional funds for its expansion. The method that the company plans on suing will have a direct effect on the value of your shares. A company issuing shares for funds will be diluting the value of the outstanding shares. The new shares will diminish the ownership percentage that your shares represent.

If the shares that the company issues are restricted the dilution will not have an effect on the outstanding shares until they become free trading. Once they are free trading the holders of those shares will be able to sell them in the market. By introducing new shares into the market the supply is increased. The price will decrease if the demand for shares is constant now that the supply has been increased.

Companies may opt to raise funds by borrowing. They issue a bond to a lender in exchange for the funds. The interest rate for a micro cap will be high due to the high risk the lender is assuming by making the loan. There is a risk that the micro cap will default on the loan due to its high interest rate, in which case the company might have to declare bankruptcy. Debt is cheaper than raising funds through equity since the interest paid on the loans is tax deductible versus dividends that are not tax deductible. Penny stocks generally do not issue dividends but they are still better off borrowing money than issuing shares.

The interest rate is tax deductible and there usually is a built safety net for both the company and the lender that helps the company avoid bankruptcy in case of default and helps the debtor recuperate his loan. In case of default the loan can be converted into stock in the company. At this point there will be major dilution of stock since the debtor receives the money owed to him in stock. But this only happens if the company defaults on the loan and has no other way to pay the loan back. This would only happen in a worst-case scenario when the debtor does not accept a smaller payment plan. In the case that the company issues shares in exchange for funds there is instant share dilution. In that case the stock would instantly be worth less due to the higher amount of shares. By borrowing money the company is not diluting shares and if it can pay back the loan it will never have to dilute shareholder ownership. Find out which method the penny stock will be using, or is currently using to raise funds.

The performance of the stock can be gauged by its past performance to a degree. You can not know how the stock will do based on past performance but you can see how the stock reacts to certain market conditions that are likely to repeat itself. Markets move in cycles, going up and down in waves that react to political and economic events. Even in this bull market there have been up and down periods. You want to look back and see how the penny stock performed in up and down periods. A stock that lost a large percentage of its value does not have a strong support base. Its investors do not believe in it enough to endure a bad market. The company might not have strong fundamentals that would allow it to persevere in a recession. Investors know this and sell the stock when the market and economy slow down. You would not want to own this stock if there is danger of having a slow down in the economy or the market, regardless of how short term it might be.

A penny stock that beats the returns of similar penny stocks in an up market means that it offers something that similar company's lack. Analyze what is attracting investors to this stock. If the attraction is a long-term factor that should continue regardless of the condition of the economy the stock should continue doing well for a while. Depending on what the factor is, it could be a monopoly in an emerging marketplace; it could fuel long-term price growth. The company has enough going for it that it might even do well in a down market.

Short sales are transactions in which shares have been borrowed from brokers and sold. The shorter must return the stock at a later point and pay interest on the value of the shares he borrowed. The shorter is hoping that the price will go down so when he buys the shares back he will have to pay less for them than what he sold them for. He profits from the difference in price from when he borrowed and sold them and the price that he buys them back to return them to the broker. The shorter is taking an immense amount of risk by engaging in this transaction. If the price doubles he will have to pay twice as much for the shares that he borrowed. Many people lost money by shorting Internet stocks that continued rising in price.

Because of the high risk that a shorter takes he puts in a great deal of research. He is almost sure beyond a doubt that the stock will go down. The shorter has years of experience shorting stocks and is usually very proficient at what he does. So when you see that a penny stock is being shorted you should ask yourself a hard why. The shorter has a strong reason for shorting the stock. The only reason you would invest a penny stock that is being shorted is because you know the reason that it is expected to fall and you disagree with the reason. If you do not know the reason stay away since you will never know if the reason is coming true. A shorter might short a penny stock because he expects it to default on a loan. You need to determine if it will default or not. If you are sure beyond a doubt that it can make payments on the loan then you can ignore the shorter. If you see that a large percentage of the stock is being shorted you should be extremely careful since it seems that there is a consensus that the stock will go down.

Companies issue additional shares for many reasons. They issue shares to compensate their employees. They issue shares as incentives for employees to take a job with the company. Shares are used to form strategic partnerships with other companies. Acquisitions are mostly done with issued shares since the cost is substantially cheaper than if the penny stock tried to buy another company with cash.

Regardless of the reason for issuing shares the end result will be share dilution. The price of the penny stock will decrease as the additional shares are sold in the market. If the penny stock will be issuing more shares make sure that the reason it is issuing the shares will bring enough of a price increase to compensate for the share dilution. Shares being used to buy a company that would double the revenues of a penny stock company are worth the share dilution as long as you the number of outstanding shares is not doubled.

Companies that trade on the OTC market do not always have small market caps. Loch Harris at one point was trading for over $5 a share giving the company more than a billion dollar market cap. There are many Nasdaq companies that have much smaller market caps. Then why would an OTC stock with a large market cap remain on the OTC when it is worth more than many Nasdaq companies?

For a company to be listed on the Nasdaq market it needs to meet many requirements in addition to attaining a stock price of over $3. Having a large market cap is not enough to be considered for a listing on the Nasdaq or on any other exchange. OTC stocks have a very hard maintaining large market caps. The price of a LOCH share retreated all the way back to .50 within a few months of the high. People realize that the company usually does not have the required fundamentals or the investor support to keep the share price over a certain amount after a run up in price. There will always be profit taking from investors after a run up in price.

Unlike stocks that are traded on the exchanges, penny stock investors are not long term investors so after they see a large gain in price they take their profits and move on. Because of this I would not invest in a penny stock with a market cap of over $100 million or a stock that has increased by more than 100% in less than a week period. The $100 million market cap is excessive for a penny stock and will result in very close SEC scrutiny of the company. The SEC wants to make sure investors are not buying up the stock of a fraudulent company. Even if the company is not doing anything wrong an SEC investigation can result in a huge loss in the value of the market cap.

Also a penny stock company with a market cap of over $100,000,000 can no longer be considered an undiscovered gem. The huge market cap will register it on everyone's radar. And by definition that stock already has large following of investors, other wise they would not have been able to bid up the price of the stock to the point where the company has its current market cap. I want to invest in penny stocks that have not been discovered by more than a handful of investors. A penny stock with that market cap most likely has a few thousand shareholders already in place. The stock is discussed every day in the message boards and the name of the company is recognizable to most penny stock investors. Unless something dramatic happens the stock will keep the current number of shareholders it now has. If people were going to buy it they would have already done so based on all the available information on the company. A penny stock with a few investors and little exposure has plenty of potential to attract new investors.

The problem with buying a stock that has risen by more than 100% in a one-week period is that there will be many investors sitting on 100%, 75%, and 50% profits. The price of the stock is at the point where they can sell and walk away with a massive gain. If I buy the stock at this point I am facing the risk that investors will start cashing in their profits after I have bought my shares. Once the profit taking starts all the early investors will sell hoping to establish their profits before the price drops to the point where they bought it.

SBID moved from .50 to $3 in 10 days based on news and exposure. The profit taking started when investors realized the gains they were sitting on. The stock retreated to .50 four days after it reached $3. Once the profit taking started everyone who stood to make a profit sold before the window of opportunity was closed.

To avoid this situation I restrict myself to buying stocks before they have moved more than 50% in a one-week period. This way if I but the stock a stock at .15 that traded at .10 the day before I can still enjoy the next 50% gain without having to worry about profit taking. From my experience investors will not take their profits until the stock has gained 100% or more unless there they see the stock being dumped, or bad news is released. Now that I have the stock at .15 I can hold it with more safety. If the stock is sold off at .30 I still have 15 cents at where I can make a profit. I can sell the stock at anywhere from .30 to .155 and make money. If the stock drops back after I buy it my loss is limited since people will start buying it since they expect the price to pick up again and finish the run. Their buying will allow me to exit my position at a small loss. If I bought the stock at .30 and everyone started selling knowing that the run is over I could find myself trying to sell the stock in a market where investors are selling and there are no buyers for the stock.

The lessons are only to buy penny stocks with market caps of under $100,000,000 and penny stocks that are trading fro less than 100% of the price they traded for the prior week.

CHAPTER 11

Investor Relations Firms

Investor relations firms are firms hired by companies to publicize their business to the public. They cannot be compensated with stock to discourage a firm from convincing investors to but the stock. The investor relations firm can talk to investors about the business of the company and the direction the company wants to head in. The firm needs to make sure that any information that it divulges to investors is already public information. The information becomes public when it is released through a press release. The investor relations firm cannot give investment advice such as recommendations to buy a stock, price performance, or suitability of a stock for the investor's portfolio. An investor relations firm is there to build relationships with the investors of the company, and to keep the investment community informed of the company's progress. The purpose of having an investor relations firm is to have a means to communicate with investors and influence them to buy the stock. Bu the influence is limited to providing them with information and letting them decide on their own over the suitability of the stock in their portfolio.

The investor relations firm plays an important role in attracting investors to a stock. The firm needs to be able to build a reputation fro open communication between it and the investors. Investors will stay with a declining stock if the IR firm explains to them why the price is going down and assures them of the long term success of the company. People make judgments on companies based on the interaction they have with the IR firm. For this reason it is very important for a penny stock to have an experienced and honest IR firm. The penny stock can have the hottest gizmo to hit the market in this century, but if investors cannot contact the IR firm to get information they will not buy the stock. The IR is to investors what customer service is to a shopper at a car dealership. You would not buy a car unless someone patiently answered all your questions and returned your calls. You want to be able to call the IR firm and have someone patiently explain to you the purpose of a new product or the effect of a new development on the company. Companies with strong IR firms will keep investors informed and interested in the stock. The investors will buy the stock and the price will rise. The opposite will take place with a firm with an unprofessional IR firm. Investors will feel insulted after having called countless times and not received a call back. They will sell the shares they have. They will not buy any shares after interacting with the irresponsible IR firm.

For this reason it is imperative that you make sure that the penny stock you are considering investing has a good IR firm. It might not be that important to you if the IR firm returns your calls or not. But I can assure you that it will be important to other investors who need more information before they buy the stock.

You can check up on the IR firm by calling them up and discussing the stock with them. See how long they are willing to stay on the phone with you. Notice the patience and knowledge they exhibit when talking to you. In order to convince potential investors to become investors the IR people will have to be enthusiastic about the client they represent.

A solid IR firm will have been in business for at least three years, or have principals who have been in business for at least 3 years. The firm should have a roster of clients that have used them for over a year. The typical client will sign up for a one-year period. If they are satisfied with the work that the IR firm has done they will continue using the firm after the one-year period is complete. You should ask the IR firm how many years their average client has used them for. You want to hear that their average client stays with them for more than a year. This would tell you that they are helping attract and maintain investors for the penny stock.

Hard working IR firms will develop a strong reputation. Their reputation will translate into having many clients. I consider having 3 or more clients a sign that the company is effective. An IR firm with 5 or more clients is effective and has developed a good reputation. An IR firm without many clients is most likely a cheaper firm that attracts companies that can only afford basic IR firms. If they had a solid reputation they would be attracting micro cap companies with the resources to pay for their excellent services. IR firms will try putting a positive spin on the reason they only have a one or two clients. They will claim that they want to devote all their energies to one company that they believe in. But regardless of how much they believe in that one company they still are in business grow profits. And growing your client base increases profits. A company with over 3,000 shareholders might elect to hire an IR firm that will exclusively work with them. But they will only sign a deal with an IR firm that has an extensive reputation. They would not risk losing their shareholders because of firm with little experience. If the IR firm tells you that the reason they are only working with one client is because of the large numbers of investors the company has, ask them for the names and numbers of past clients. They will give you the names and numbers if they have nothing to hide. Call the references and establish if they were satisfied with the IR firm and the reason they no longer use them.

You will come across press releases from IR firms announcing a termination of services for a company. This termination can take place for various reasons. The company might be experiencing a cash crunch and can no longer pay for the IR services, or they received a better price from another firm. I tend to believe that companies do not release IR firms for this reason.

If they are suffering a cash crunch they can arrange a payment plan until they are back on their feet. If they really are hurting financially you do not want to invest in the company altogether. As far as switching to another firm because of a lower price, I find that reason just as hard to believe. When the IR firm leaves the company, all the relationships it has developed with the media and investors on the penny stock's behalf are now out the lost to the company. The new IR firm will be unfamiliar to investors and will take time to adjust to the new company. Investors will expect the same relationship they had with the old IR firm. When they do not have that relationship and the access to information it entailed, they will sell their stock and move on to another penny stock.

Companies know that it is in their best interest to work with one IR firm for as long as they are in business. They will only terminate their relationship with the IR firm if they are forced to do so. Sometimes IR firms overstep their bounds out of eagerness to promote the company. They release insider information ahead of time. The management finds this out and is faced with a dilemma.

Management wants to continue using the IR firm but knows that the IR firm has violated securities law. The SEC can punish the IR firm and the penny stock for violating inside information rules. The company needs to fire the IR firm at this point to show the SEC that they never authorized the release of information to a select few investors. By firing the firm they are distancing themselves from the actions of the investor relations firm. They can legitimately claim to the SEC that as soon as they found out about the violation they stopped using the services of the IR firm. The company would have to release the firm before any SEC investigation is initiated to show the SEC in any possible investigation that they terminated the relationship out of their volition due to the fact that they were upset with the actions of the firm.

Investor relation firms will also terminate relationships they have with paying clients under certain circumstances. An IR firm will terminate a relationship with the penny stock when it suspects the company of wring doing. The IR firm does not wan to have its name associated with a penny stock that later on become the focus of an investigation. To avoid this the IR firms will research their clients before taking them on. This does not mean that they will not take on a client with a useless product or service. Their job is to explain to the investment community and to the media why the product or service is effective and why the company has the potential to be triumphant.

It does mean that the IR firm will not take on a client who could drag it into trouble. It does not want the SEC to investigate it along with the penny stock for possible fraud. In a situation where the IR firm has reasons to believe that there is something wrong taking place it will terminate the relationship. It will send out a press release informing the investment community that they will no longer be representing the penny stock. Sometimes the company will try to send out a press release first saying that they are no longer suing the IR firm to make it seem as if it was their choice to terminate the relationship. You should call both the company and the IR firm to determine why the relationship has been severed. They will both try to make themselves look good so it is up to you to ask hard questions and read between the lines. How they say what they say could be more important than what they say.

Penny stocks that do not have a full time IR firm or IR person are sending out the message that investors are not their main priority. If you call them they will tell you that their focus is on building the company and increasing profits, not increasing the price of the stock. That is good from the perspective of management, which has been hired to grow the business and increase profits. But it is a bad attitude to have as far as investors are concerned. Investors make money when the stock price goes up, not when the company makes money. Penny stocks do not have pay dividends, so there is no promise of receiving a share of the profits.

I have had this argument with the management of penny stock companies very often. They feel that as the business grows the price of the stock will follow. This is nonsense. The price of the stock will only go up if investors buy the stock. A company can earn half a billion dollars in one quarter, but if investors decide never to buy a single share the stock of the company will be worth zero. The flip side is true; if investors decide to buy stock in a company that has no earnings the price of the stock will go up. It does not matter to investors that the business is not growing, once they decide to buy the stock it will go up. Look at all the Internet stocks without any earnings that have billion dollar valuations. My point is that prices do not move in tandem with the performance of the company. If management of a company wants their stock to increase in price they need to publicize their company. The only effective way to publicize your company to investors is by hiring a full time IR person or by hiring an investor relations firm.

I can think of many great penny stocks that languish in darkness because of the lack of exposure they receive. I remember a great company that traded for under .20 for months until it received exposure on a national talk show. Once it was featured on the talk show the stock moved above .50. The product and company had not changed. The only thing that had changed was the exposure that the company received.

Make sure that the penny stock you are going to invest in either has an IR person or is in the process of hiring one. The CEO cannot be the contact person for investors if he is occupied with managing the company. Especially if the company does expect to receive exposure they will need someone who can be on the phone the entire day speaking to investors. If the company is simply not concerned with its stock price then why bother investing in it.

Investor relation firms that issue excessive press releases are focused on the short term. They are working at a very fast pace to publicize their company in that period. Instead of spending time building up relationships with potential investors the firm is rushing to get the word out. You should ask your self why the firm is working so hard to get out exposure for the penny stock. If the company has long-term prospects the company would want to develop long-term investors. By sending press releases every month the company is building expectancy from investors to continue issuing press releases at a set pace. When a company starts issuing press releases every few days investors will grow accustomed to seeing that number of press releases every month. When the press releases low down investors will take the slow down as a sign that the company is slowing down. They will sell their holdings since they have no desire to hold stock in a company that is slowing down.

By sending out a small but steady number of press releases every month investors know what to expect. They feel satisfied with the information they receive from the company. A lull in press releases will not alarm them since they know that the company has been reliable in the past in releasing information. A company that starts out by sending out 4 or 5 press releases a month cannot have a lull in issuing information. The investors on that company are not used to going through a week without some news being presented by the company. Eventually when this lull comes investors will sell the stock since they will become worried at the sudden pause in press releases. A company that only sends out one or two releases a month can go without sending a press release for three weeks without alarming investors.

Another danger of investing in a penny stock that sends out an excessive amount of press releases is that investors will soon start ignoring the releases. Investors will grow used to always seeing news sent out by the penny stock. And since investors know that it is not possible for a company to always have breath taking developments they will recognize the excessive releases as simply fluff. Fluff is a term used to refer for releases that simply state facts of little value to investors. Releases that pertain to an award received by an executive for an outside of the job event are useless to investors. Do you really care if the company treasure received an award from the local bowling league?

You would be surprised at the number of press release sent out by companies to simply see their name on a release. They send out the press releases to keep their name on news wires. They are doing the equivalent of a political campaign posting stickers on lampposts. The purpose of the stickers is to register the candidate's name in voters' heads. After a while voters tune out the name of the candidate since they have been overtly exposed to it and now annoyed. Investors become equally annoyed when they see a penny stock issuing one empty release after another. Everyone knows the story of the boy who cried wolf. The boy keeps telling the villagers that he saw a wolf. They rightfully ignore him until he really see a wolf and then is ignored by the disbelieving villagers. When the company has something serious to say investors will not pay attention to it because they have already decided to ignore the company.

A lack of press releases is just as dangerous as an excessive amount of press releases is. Investors need to be informed about the developments the penny stock is undergoing. Most investors will not call up companies for information. They rely on the issuance of press releases to obtain information. If they do not see any press releases they will come to the conclusion that nothing is going at the company. If they have not bought the penny stock they will not have any reason to do so. Why would they buy the stock of a company that is not aggressively engaged in business? There are plenty of other penny stocks issuing press releases. No one will buy the stock of a company that does not release information when there are plenty of companies that do release information on a timely basis.

Investors in a penny stock that is not issuing information will sell their shares. They will understand the lack of information as a sign that the company has lost its track. They bought the stock for a reason but will now assume that the reason is no longer valid. If the company were still in the same direction they would be updated periodically via a press release.

Just as important as making sure that the penny stock you want to invest in sends out press releases you want to make sure that the releases are not too frequent or tardy. Consistency is vital to build up long-term investors. For a penny stock to be come a dollar stock it will need long term investors who do not cash out and new investors who buy in and hold the stock for the long term. The IR firm can attract long-term investors if its focus is also long term.

IR firms are important for the price of the stock. They influence the price of the stock by attracting and maintaining investor
interest. Simply put, the more investors who the IR firm can convince to come on board and stay on board, the higher the price of
the stock will go. We have already discussed how bad investor
relations firms can turn off investors and discourage potential investors from buying the stock. We also discussed how to look into
the professionalism and ability of an IR firm. What we now need
to discuss is how to find an IR firm that is effective in being able to
increase the value of the stock price.

There are many IR firms that can keep the investment community abreast of corporate developments. They receive high rat-
ings from the clients they service. But as an investor you need
more than what the company needs. A company might be happy
with an IR firm that ensures that it receives enough exposure to
keep the stock price at the current price. The penny stock might
be interested in showing institutional investors that the price is
stable and it is a good long-term investment. The company might
not even care what the price of its stock is. It can be using an IR
firm that specializes in developing a company image and not on
developing interest in the stock.

That type of IR firm would be useless for you as an investor.
You need the stock to increase in price. You want the price of the
stock to move up, while the CEO of the above mentioned company might only want to develop an image that would allow him
to do business for elite nonprofit institutions. While you are sweat-
ing over the performance of the stock the CEO is only focused on
being perceived as a company that can do business with the most
prestigious organizations in the country.

You need to invest in penny stocks that are using IR firms that
have proven in the past their ability to increase shareholder value.
You can find out what their goal by simply asking them what their
intentions are for the company stock. If they tell you that their
objective is to concentrate more on the company image and hope
that as a by product of their efforts the stock will go up, then you

are out of luck. This IR firm will let the stock price languish out of their concern for the image of the company. You want an IR firm that has been hired specifically to increase shareholder value.

Once you have found a penny stock with an IR firm bent on increasing the price of the stock you are ready for the next step. You need to find out what their track record is. You want to make sure that the IR firm is capable of increasing the market cap of the company. Just because the IR firm wants the price of the stock it does not meant that they will be successful. Remember, this IR firm is in a very delicate situation. It wants the price of the stock to go up but it cannot recommend the purchase of the stock. A recommendation of the stock would result in the wrath of the SEC, which insists that registered and licensed individuals make investment recommendations. An IR frim is not a registered financial advisor or a broker.

The IR firm will have to excite investors of the prospects of the company without urging them to become shareholders or promising a future increase in the price of the stock. The IR firm can discuss the current actions of the penny stock and discuss the future plans. Effective IR firms use investor packages and newsletters to build credibility and excitement for their clients. Their aim is that once investors receive all the information on the company along with a summary on the market and the potential profits that are available investors will buy the stock on their own.

You can see how good an IR firm is at increasing the value of a stock by looking at the performance of the stock of their other clients. You can ask the IR firm for the date they signed on the client and the date they terminated the contract. Use a chart for that period and see how the stock performed.

You might notice that some IR firms are able to initially increase the price of the stock when they first take on a client and then the price stays dormant for the duration of the IR firm's work for the company. This is due to the excitement generated by the PR firm announcing that they are now working with the company. After the excitement dies down investors move on to other stocks.

If the IR firm has this effect on penny stocks it works with you would only buy the stock when they sign up the client and sell the stock as the excitement peaks.

There are IR firms that increase the long-term price of the stock by means of their active promotion work. The IR understands what makes a penny stock appreciate in value and what its role in bringing up the price of the stock is. By looking at an IR firm's track record you can approximate the effect it will have for the penny stock that they have taken on as a new client.

There are other factors besides the ability of an IR firm that contribute to the performance of a stock. A company headed for bankruptcy will see a loss in price in its stock no matter how good their IR firm is. The IR firm can try to salvage the image of the company but investors will sell the stock since it is headed for bankruptcy.

On the other hand sometimes a stock performs very well without the aid of its IR firm. A company that developed a cure for cancer would not need the assistance of an IR firm to encourage people to become investors. The media would swamp the company with enough attention to draw thousands of investors on board.

While finding the cure for cancer is a dramatic example, there are examples of corporate developments that would lead to an increase in price without the aid of an investor relations firm. A penny stock that has increased its revenues by 300% would see its stock move up as long as a press release was issued. The IR firm would not need to cleverly word the release. Just the release of the revenue increase would be enough to draw investor interest.

You need to make sure that you do not give an IR firm credit for increasing the price of stock when they had nothing to do with it. Every IR firm will take the credit for an increase in its clients' stock price. But if you want to pick IR firms based on their ability to increase the price of their clients' stock you will need to make sure that there is a connection between the work of the IR firm and the performance of the stock.

CHAPTER 12

Negative Situations

There are negative situations and events that can adversely affect the price of the stock. This chapter will teach you to be able to discern negative situations that are developing. By reading this chapter you will recognize events that can negatively impact the value of a penny stock.

Companies looking to bring up the price of their shares will often resort to doing reverse splits. In a reverse split the number of shares are reduced by a pre-selected factor. The ownership stake of the shares remains the same. A company having a 100 for 1 reverse split is diminishing the number of outstanding shares by 100. The new number of shares outstanding is now 100 times less than it previously was. The new share still retains the ownership percentage that 100 shares previously did. The price of the new stock reflects the number of shares it has taken the place of. If the old stock was worth .03 the new stock will be worth $3.00 since it is comprised of 100 old shares. You are now holding 1000 shares valued at $3000 where before you were holding 100,000 shares valued at $3,000. Your cost basis for the shares is still the same and the value of the shares will initially be the same.

The problem is that investors do not have faith that the stock will retain the higher price. They know that the stock is a penny stock with penny stock fundamentals. The company has not developed to the point where the stock would naturally reach the $3 price range. Investors start selling the stock, causing other investors to sell their stock, resulting in what is 90% of the time a large price decrease.

The other reason that investors start selling the stock is because they know that the company now will be issuing more
shares into the market. The company has fewer shares outstanding so it can issue more shares. The shares are also worth more
money now so the company will quickly move to take advantage
of the opportunity to use their higher valued stock. The former
penny stock can now issue 10,000 shares for allot more than it
could before. The shares can be used to make acquisitions and
allow the company not to have use as many shares as it would
have had to in the past. The new shares that are used will further
dilute the number of outstanding share in the market and bring
down the price.

You should never buy or hold a stock that has announced or
will soon be announcing a reverse split. There is a chance that the
stock could increase in value after the split if the company has an
outstanding development that provides a reason to support the
higher price. But from experience at least 9 out of 10 reverse splits
will force down the price of the stock. With all the other opportunities that can be found in penny stocks why invest in a penny
stock that will most likely go down in price.

Penny stocks that are in bankruptcy will drastically fluctuate
in price as the bankruptcy process moves on. The price fluctuation
results from investors misunderstanding the bankruptcy process.
When they hear that the company has obtained bankruptcy protection they assume that it means that the company is now protected against further financial harm. All bankruptcy protection
means is that the company cannot be pursued by creditors and
that a repayment plan will either be set up or the company will be
reorganized. The company can still be liquidated if it no longer
has the cash to operate. Or the bankrupt company can simply
cease doing business and close up shop. Caldor filed for bankruptcy and then moved on to be liquidated. The stock trades on
the pink sheets for .001 a share down from the .50 price range
when it first announced that it had filed bankruptcy. Public companies, like private businesses, after going bankrupt often cease

doing business instead of trying to reorganize. Once they cease doing business their stock is worthless.

In my opinion, the reorganization process is never favorable towards equity investors. This means that even if the company announces that it will be reorganizing and emerging from bankruptcy equity holders can still lose their entire investment. Reorganizations shift ownership of the company into the hands of the creditors and bondholders, leaving the common stock holders with nothing. Sometimes common equity holders receive a small stake in the new company. The new ownership stake of the old common equity holders will consist of either a very small stake in the company or warrants to buy the new stock.

The reason this happens is because bondholders and creditors receive proceeds from the liquidation of the company before common equity holders do. The stockholders will only be compensated after the bondholders and creditors have received the money owed to them. But since in a bankruptcy the bondholders and creditors will have to settle for as low as .20 on the dollar, there is no money left over for common stock holders.

Many investors think that reorganization means that they will receive stock in the new company. They buy the stock since they believe that they are buying into a turn around situation. Unfortunately they are mistaken and soon lose their entire investment.

Micro cap companies vary in the products and services that they offer. Many micro cap companies focus on standard products and established markets. Numerous micro caps focus on new untested products and what they perceive as being new emerging markets. When deciding on which micro cap to invest you in you want to be able to research the market for the product. The newer and untested the product is the harder it will be research its potential.

A new product is fine as long as its market is established. A new computer device can be profitable if there already is a market for it. But the same computer product would not be a hit in a country with a very low computer usage rate. Make sure that there is a demand for the penny stock's product.

Many micro caps have products for which they plan on creating a market for. They might develop a device that can detect when milk is spoiled. While people might be concerned with being able to know if the milk is spoiled or not, they can resort to the old-fashioned smell test. This product although advanced and useful would have no practical market since people do not need a device to measure the freshness of milk. The company would have to convince people somehow that they are better off using a $10 device for an action that they can do for free now. I am sure you can see how quickly both the product and company would fail.

Be wary of investing in penny stocks that sell products that are not tested and for which there is no demand. People buy products that fill a need. They do not products when they do not have a need for them.

Hot tips are a source of trouble. Investors receive hot tips from friends, relatives, and business associates. The tip itself is not the problem. Very often the tips are valuable and the stock's they concern do go up. The problem with hot tips is that most often by the time you get it the whole world has had time to react to the same information you were given. The information originates from an original source that passes the tip down to a few selected individuals who pass it down to their friends who pass it on again until the full cycle is repeated. The issue that I have with hot tips is that you never know how far down you are in the chain. If you are the 100th person to receive the tip chances are that the stock has already been bought up and the price reflects the information. If the tip comes out to be true there will be selling from the investors who bought the stock before you. By the time you buy it people might be getting ready to sell the stock.

The other problem with buying a stock based on a hot tip is that you are deviating from your investment strategy. You are not buying the stock based on your research and your money is at the mercy of a tip that may be wrong. You can make the right investments based on your research without having to rely on other people's advice.

If you are offered inside information you will be highly tempted to act on it. I am warning you now that if the SEC discovers that you have traded based on inside information they will be merciless. I remember reading about a group of 20 people who were penalized by the SEC for trading based on inside information. The group of 20 people did not consist of high-powered Wall Street players. They were a group of doctors, lawyers, secretaries, and relatives who were barely connected to each other. A lawyer working on a merger passed information to his doctor who passed on a tip to his secretary who told her husband who told his friends and so on. By the time the information had passed though the chain 20 people had acted on the inside information. The SEC forced everyone to repay the profits they had made plus substantial penalties.

Inside information does not pay at the end. If you have received inside information on a company do not buy the stock even if you planned to buy it for another reason altogether. The Securities Exchange Commission will view your trade in connection to the inside information it suspects you of having received.

Government investigations always have adverse effects on penny stocks. The investigation can conclude with the company being cleared. But by the time the company is cleared and the investigation is complete the name of the company will have been dragged through the mud. Investors will read about what the reason the government is investigating the company and assume that the penny stock is guilty as charged. Penny stocks have a bad reputation to begin with so it will not take much to ruin the reputation of a penny stock.

I would not invest in the stock of a penny stock being investigated. For starters, the government has some of the brightest minds working for it. If they find a reason to open an investigation they more than likely have an excellent reason for doing so. And even if the investigation does not turn anything up it will take months if not years for the price to recover.

Consumer backlash against a company is even worse than a government investigation. A government investigation will either

find the company guilty or innocent of the suspected wrongdo-
ing. Once a company has been found to be innocent investors will
slowly return. It can take years for them to come back but there is
nothing preventing them from returning to the stock. Consumer
backlash against a company is enormously damaging both to the
company and to the stock. When consumers decide that they no
longer trust the quality of a product or the competence of the
company they will never use its products again. A company that
manufactures defective car seats will never be able to over come the
stigma resulting from an accident. Customers will never take a
chance with their car seats because of what is at stake. The company will not sell any more car seats and its stock will crumble
when earnings turn into losses.

Micro cap companies that are the focus of customer backlash
do not have the benefit of sitting on a cushion of cash to help them
pass through the difficult period. A large established company has
enough cash to weather a storm. The micro cap cannot count on a
press relations department to work the media. Once it becomes
embroiled in a customer backlash period it can start counting its
days.

The old-fashioned boiler room operation consisted of a row of
phones manned by brokers with the job of calling investors and
convincing them to buy a worthless a stock. The stock would appreciate in price and the boiler room operator would dump his
shares to the unsuspecting investors. Boiler room victims were usually the elderly who are unfamiliar to investing and are by nature
more trusting.

Today the boiler room operation has substituted the use of
phones for the Internet. The Internet provides the tools to reach
millions of investors with the push of a button. In the time that it
used to take to call one investor, the boiler room operation can
now send an email touting a stock to thousands of investors.

Other ways stocks are sold to unsuspecting investors under
false premises is through the use of newsletters, emails, message
boards, and chat rooms. A thinly traded stock is first bought up

by a group of investors. Once they control the supply the start promoting it using every available means. The stock price increases sharply due to the lack of supply since the group controls the supply. Investors continue placing orders for the stock that is being marked up by the market makers due to the high demand and limited supply. When the stock is high enough the group dumps all their shares on the investors who soon discover that the information on the stock was fabricated and that the stock was manipulated.

CHAPTER 13

Investment Strategies

The following chapter discusses investment and trading strategies that can be effectively applied to penny stocks. The following strategies will be helpful if you have become experienced in understanding and practicing the proceeding chapters. You should read over the following strategies a few times over. After reading the strategies and becoming familiar with them you should select the strategy that fits your tolerance for risk. The strategy should fit your over all investment philosophy and preferably match up with your skills. Some people prefer long-term strategies to short term strategies. The following strategies entail a great deal or risk. But like the saying goes, no pain no gain.

Strategy #1

Buy stocks that are being used for reverse mergers. When a company that has no operations announces that it will be acquiring a private company and then changing its name to the name of the private company, it is undergoing a reverse merger. In the reverse merger, the private company is being taken over by the public company. Once the public company takes over the private company, it transfers a majority of the shares of the company to the private company. Since the private company now has a majority of the shares it now controls the public company. In effect, although the private company was taken over by the penny stock, the owners of the private company now own the penny stock. They have merged their business with the penny stock and now are the majority shareholders of the penny stock.

The following information is based in part on information from the Venturea.com web site. The site is operated by Venture Associates, a consulting firm that arranges reverse mergers and financing for private businesses wishing to go public.

There are advantages to doing a reverse merger with a public company. A reverse merger takes less time compared to an IPO. An IPO requires extensive paperwork that can take up to a year to file while a reverse merger can be done in a matter of months.

A reverse merger also saves considerable money. The cost of the shell is under $200,000 including lawyer fees. The cost of an IPO can start at $750,000 excluding the underwriter fees.

The business owner can raise money privately before the registration and can sell shares to the public after the registration is completed.

The shares can be used for acquisitions. The public company can now use its shares to acquire other business and grow through acquisitions. A private business is limited in its ability to buy other existing businesses to the cash on hand or to the access it has to financing. By going public, the same business can use its stock to buy a business that is for sale. The seller receives a liquid security that can further appreciate in value while the cost to the buyer is only his original cost to purchase the shell. If the buyer paid $200,000 for the shell, and now 3 months later the shell is worth $500,000 his cost basis is still only $200,000. He can use 10% of his stock to acquire a $50,000 business without having to spend $50,000. The 10% of his company that he is exchanging for the private business will only cost him $20,000 based on the 10% of the total purchase price of the shell. Companies that have used reverse mergers to go public will build up their business before making acquisitions. By building up their business they can increase the price of their stock and leverage its value in further acquisitions.

The reason that investors will sell a shell to a private company is because they receive upwards of $100,000 in cash for the stock and they keep a minimum of 5% of the stock in the post merger company.

The shells, or penny stocks, that private companies use to go public do not have any ongoing operations. They are referred to as shells because their only reason for existing is to be used for a merger. Therefore, the price of stock that is nothing but a shell is very low. The price of a penny stock that is used for a reverse merger is often below .10. The stock starts appreciating in price once the public company announces that it has acquired a private company. Investors now will value the shell according to the operations of the business that is has merged with. If the private company has a strong product that is in demand investors will start buying shares of the company sending the price up. The shareholders who sold the shell now own 5% of a stock that has value and the buyers of the shell now can raise money using their appreciating stock.

The investors who buy in early can benefit from the price appreciation that will result as investors realize that the penny stock is no longer a shell but is now an operating business. If the private company has earnings, the stock will appreciate much faster due to the intrinsic value of the stock and the scarcity of profitable penny stocks. A profitable penny stock will stand out from most penny stocks. This penny stock has revenues and earnings while most penny stocks are still at the stage where they are developing their product.

By buying early and holding stocks used for reverse mergers you are buying a worthless stock that now owns a valuable asset. By definition, the valuable asset will increase the worth of the cheap stock. I bought BMKS, before it changed its name to reflect the merger with the private company it acquired, for less than .15. Before the merger, the penny stock did not interest anyone since it was only a shell. Once it acquired and merged with a private company it became a real business with operations. Within a few months the stock rose to over a $1 based on the progress and existing operations of the private company.

Strategy # 2

Using the same reasoning for buying a penny stock undergoing a reverse merger you should also focus on buying stocks that can be used for reverse mergers. These are penny stocks that have low floats and low market caps. There are dealers who specialize in providing shells for private businesses. You can still buy shares of the shell on the open market since the dealer will not own all of the available shares. Or the management of a company will send out a press release announcing that they are currently have no operations and are looking to enter into acquire an ongoing business.

You can read this information in the quarterly reports that public companies file with the SEC. Management needs to provide an overview of the company and they will often state that they are looking to use their status as public company to acquire a private business. AMDI is a shell with no operations. It files all of its quarterly and annual reports stating that they are looking to acquire an ongoing business. The stock has increased in price from as low as .02 to as high as .20 based on speculation on the value of the stock once it is used to for a reverse merger.

The penny stock might never be used for a reverse merger in which case it could return to the .01 price range or a Chinese company wanting to go public may use the stock and the price could rise to $4 like YNOT did.

Strategy # 3

Buy low and sell high. Penny stocks have their peaks and valleys like all major stocks. The difference is that stocks on established exchanges usually move in one direction in the long term. They can swing in price from $40 to $50 but eventually will either rise above $50 or head below $40. A penny stock can repeat the cycle numerous times without breaking out of its annual high and low. The reason this occurs is because penny stock investors start taking

their profits when the stock appreciates above 100%, and finish
taking their profits when the stock reaches its high. They figure
that they can make money at this point so why should they risk
their money by holding a stock that could lose 50% of its value in
an hour.

Every time the stock reaches its high there will be heavy selling from profit takers and investors who do not think that the
stock can break its high. The selling drives down the price until
the stock reaches its low and investors consider it a bargain. Once
the stock is at its low penny stock investors rationalize that it is a
good buy since it cannot move any lower. They look at the difference in price between the high and the low, which can be as much
as $4 sometimes, and encouraged by the upside potential they
start buying up the stock. Other investors see the buying and the
price increase that the buying causes and they decide to buy. They
look at the high and realize that the stock has plenty of room to go
up and continue buying it until the price is near the high. At the
point that the stock reaches its high investors start selling again
repeating the process. The stock needs to have good news to encourage investors to buy in the first place, but after the investors
have bought the stock they will use the high and low for the year
to determine a good entry and exit point.

If you want to take advantage of this opportunity you should
look for penny stocks that have been trading at their 52-week
low. You want to make sure that the penny stock is still not in
the process of dropping so make sure to buy a stock that has
been sitting at the low for a few weeks. Then call the company
and find out if there will be any developments that could trigger
investors to start buying the stock again. If there is a positive
development you will benefit immensely from having bought
the stock at its all time low. If the positive news does not lift the
price you can sell the stock a week later for almost the same price
you bought it at.

Strategy # 4

Buy a penny stock that has sustained a high. Most penny stocks after reaching their 52-week high will experience a wave of selling. The wave of selling would not take place if investors believed that there was more to come and that soon the price would be even higher. Their expectancy could be based on a deal that is being worked on or on a contract that the company has just received. The stock will then establish a new base at the high as investors hold their stock and wait to see what happens next. If the company continues growing they will hold the stock and add on to their positions. When the stock crosses over its 52-week high other investors will notice and buy the penny stock. They will buy the stock based on the rationale that if the stock was able to break through its 52-week ceiling the stock will continue going up and establish a new 52-week high. You can profit from this anticipation by buying penny stocks that have reached their 52-week high and maintained their price. By buying the penny stock you have the potential of owning a penny stock that will be attracting interest from all the investors who expect it to establish a new 52-week high. The risk is that the selling might only be delayed and that it will start once the stock is one or two cents above its annual high. To minimize this risk wait at least 4 days before buying the stock to see if it stabilizes. If the price starts declining after you buy it immediately sell your position and move on. Once the selling starts the stock could easily retreat to anywhere between its 52-week high and low.

Strategy # 5

Dollar Averaging. Dollar averaging is the practice of buying more shares of a stock that you own as the price declines. You are lowering your average cost per share by buying the stock at a lower price. When the stock rebounds you will be establishing an over all profit on all of your shares. For example, you own 10,000 shares of a .10 stock that drops to .05 in bad week. Instead of liquidating your position at a loss you buy 10,000 more shares at .05. Your average cost per share is now .075. You now only need the stock to rebound back to .08 to make a profit on your entire investment. If the stock does move beyond .10 based on the original reason you bought the first 10,000 shares, you will have an average cost of .075 and a higher profit than if you had bought all of your shares at .10.

The risk is that the stock will continue heading south and all you have done is throw good money after bad money. I am not in favor averaging down. The only way I would consider averaging down is if the stock dropped and is now to starting to recover. Depending on the rate of recovery I could conclude that the stock should be shortly above the price where I bought it. By buying the stock then I am locking in a profit as the stock moves up, which brings me to my next strategy.

Strategy # 6

Buying on a dip. Penny stocks can have short-term dips in price for various reasons. The price can dip because of the poor performance of a similar stock or as a result of a bad over all week for the OTC market. A dip is defined not solely as a price decrease, but as a price decrease followed by a recovery. When the stock starts recovering the proceeding drop can be considered a dip. Dips are great opportunities to buy penny stocks at. The price has temporarily dropped below its normal trading range and has now started recovering. You can but the stock for 40% below its normal trading range as it starts recovering and sell it a day later for its normal trading price. But to get a dip right you need to make sure that the reason the price dropped is because either of an unrelated event or a because of a short term negative event. Many penny stocks drop in increments, steady for a few days, and then drop in price again. They usually are dropping because of heavy profit taking or because of an adverse event. Make sure that the penny stock you are looking at has not lost value die to the above reasons. To safeguard yourself and ensure that the stock is now headed back up and that it will not just sit at that reduced price for a while make sure that the price is starting to recover. Do not let your greed convince you to rush in early. If you miscalculate you can be in for a big surprise when the stock continues heading down after a small run up. Make sure that the run up is a genuine recovery by waiting for the stock to move up 20%. Once it has moved up 20% and it is till on an up tick then it is time for you to get in. Remember why you got in to the stock. When the stock reaches back its normal trading range take your profit and start looking for your next investment.

Strategy # 7

Buy stocks with small floats and low market caps. Buying a stock with a small float and low market cap enables you to capture a large percentage of the available supply at a minimal cost. When the stock starts attracting large investor interest you will be holding a large percentage of the supply. The way the laws of supply and demand work means that the stock will appreciate much faster than a stock with a larger float under those circumstances. Also if the stock someday becomes listed on an exchange, by owning at least 5% of the company you will be entitled to special rights associated with owning art least 5% of a public company. You should be able to use your shares to vote for and against proposals and to take a board seat on the company. The challenge is finding a company with a low float and cheap stock price that has great potential so you can acquire at least 5% of the outstanding shares.

Strategy # 8

Buy pink sheet stocks. Stocks trading on the pinks are trading on the lowest market on the totem pole. They do not file financials and are not reporting. Historically, pink sheet quotes have been available through the National Quotation Bureau. They can now be accessed through certain financial web sites. You will not get a bid and ask quote but you can see the price the last trade went through at and if it was a buy or sell. You can access pink sheet quotes through Bloomberg.com and through Freerealtime.com. When using Freerealtime.com you need to add a period followed by an f to see the quote for a pink sheet stock. (MVEE.F)

There is a scarcity of information about pink sheet companies making it very difficult to research the company. Even if the CEO of the pink sheet company mails you out an investor information package it is almost impossible to verify the information. You cannot compare the information she sent you out to the annual report they filed with the SEC because pink sheet stocks do not file quarterly or annual reports.

You can still find some appealing investment opportunities in pink sheet stocks. For one, many pink sheet stocks were de-listed from the OTC for failure to file the latest financials. You can read the last financial, call the company, and try to determine why they did not file their latest financials. If the company had a temporary set back but has now filed their latest financial they could be back on the OTC market in a month or two. It might be worth holding on to the stock for a couple of months if it lost a large percentage of its value after being de-listed from the OTC. You have the opportunity to hold the stock if its value increases to its prior levels once it is re-listed on the OTC market.

Pink sheet stocks that have never filed before and have always traded on the pink sheets can make for exciting investments if you tread carefully. The market caps of those pink sheets are usually very low when compared to the market cap of similar companies trading on the OTC market. Because of the lack of information, financials, large spreads between the price you can buy them at and sell them at, and liquidity problems, investors do not like to invest in pink sheet stocks. This lack of desire for pink sheet stocks from investors results in pink sheet stocks trading for very cheap prices. A pink sheet stock that I have been following made an acquisition of a private computer business. The stock, IDFR, has remained trading between .07- .12 since the acquisition. I believe that if an OTC stock had made the same acquisition investors would have been all over the stock and the price would have climbed above .20 the month of the announcement and past .40 within two months. The problem is that because of all the earlier reasons investors do not like to buy pink sheet stocks unless there is an out of the ordinary reason. This is where your education comes into play. Once you learn how to properly research and invest in pink sheet stocks you will be able to take advantage of these opportunities.

I think that we both agree that if the pink sheet stock was trading on the OTC market the price would be allot higher. The problem is that the stock is stuck on the pink sheets so no wants to touch it with ten-foot pole. But what if the company planned on becoming fully reporting and listing on the OTC? Wouldn't the stock appreciate in value? What if the company actually was listed on the OTC wouldn't the stock move even higher?

You need to determine if the company is planning on becoming fully reporting. If they are, call them up and discern how serious they are about their plans for becoming reporting. What is their time frame for becoming fully reporting? Then ask yourself if you are willing to hold on to the stock for that period of time. If the stock is listed on the OTC and the business they have acquired is successful the stock could have the potential to become a dollar stock a year from now.

You should research pink sheet stocks the way you would research an OTC stock by following all the instructions set out in this book. In addition to the methods used for researching an OTC stock you need to insist on visiting the company. You need to visit the company headquarters and order the company's products. Find out as much as you can about the company by looking through public records. Make photocopies of every document mentioning the company and collect articles from local newspapers covering the company. Checking legal records is a must since you never know what a pink sheet company can be hiding. You can always find out if there are any major legal issues involving an OTC company by reading their filings, but there are no filings for pink sheet stocks so you need to keep digging until you have exhausted every source of information.

Once you have found a pink sheet company that you are eager to invest in expect to be patient. The company is probably under no deadlines to move ahead so you will have to wait to see if the reason you invested in the company comes to fruition. Make sure you develop a relationship with the employees of the pink sheet stock since they will be your only source of positive and negative information. If you call one morning and the secretary whispers to you that her boss has started firing most of the employees you know that it is time to sell your stock. Or you might call one afternoon and be told by an overjoyed sales agent that they have finally won a contract from General Motors worth millions of dollars. You will only be provided this information if you have developed a relationship. The old warning about inside information still applies here so make sure you do not trade on any inside information.

To leave you with a taste of what you can achieve by investing in pink sheet stocks let me tell you about stock I recently followed. OKTI announced that they were making two acquisitions and that they would make another announcement once the acquisitions are closed. The news did not move the price because of the general feelings that investors have towards penny stocks. The price remained at .07 for a week or so from which it slowly climbed to .16 over a three-week period. At this point the spread between the bid and ask was about six cents. The company then announced that they were making a third acquisition, followed by the closing of one acquisition, followed again one week later by an announcement that the second acquisition was closed. The price is now at .60 only a month after the first press release. This is the type of return that builds wealth. Find two of these stocks a year and you can place on order for your favorite Lincoln.

Strategy # 9

Always use limit orders when placing an order for penny stocks. This is not so much of a strategy but an important trading rule you should never violate. A limit order is an order to buy or sell securities in which you specify the price you want the transaction done at. The market maker can sell you the shares at a lower price than what you want them at or sell them to you for less than what you want to buy them at. By placing a limit order you protect yourself. You want this protection in a situation in which you placed an order for shares of a penny stock. You could have placed the order for 50,000 shares of a stock that was trading at .50 when you called the order in. But by the time the order has been processed the stock could be up to .75. The order will still be processed for the 50,000 shares and you will owe $12,500 because they sold you the shares at .25 more than you wanted to buy them at. They will charge you interest on the money they had to extend to cover your purchase and liquidate your holdings within a week if you do not send them a check for the amount the loaned your account.

You can place an order to sell the same 50,000 shares at the market, .50, but the market maker sees the large sell order and decides to lower his bid to .40. You have just lost $10,000 because you allowed the market maker to buy your shares at what ever priced he decided he wanted to pay for them. This is like owning a store and allowing your customers to pay whatever price they want for your merchandise. You would never do this as a seller or as customers so do not do this when you are a buyer or seller in the stock market. Always use limit orders so you are protected from price swings. This is even more important when you are placing an order for a stock with little or no volume. The market maker will have time to study your order and play with the price so he can see how high you are willing to buy and how low you are willing to sell. If you place a market order he will take the liberty of moving the price to the point where he can make the most money off you. I once an order for 5000 shares of a .10 stock get filled at .75 a share. Do not let this happen to you.

Strategy # 10

Specialize in an area that you have a natural interest in. By focusing in an area that you understand you will have a much easier
time learning about the company and its product. I would recommend that architects should specialize in penny stocks that deal
with architecture and building. As an architect you will understand the construction market and will have an instinct for the
success of a product or service in the construction market. The
same is true if you are a doctor. By investing in penny stocks that
are involved in producing medicine you will know if there is a
need for the medicine and if the company is qualified to produce
the medicine that they claim to be producing.

There are situations in which a field or a company interests
you but you have no comprehension of what is involved. I will be
the first person to admit that I have no understanding of medical
issues. Without the guidance of my parents, who are both in the
medical profession, I would not know the difference between a
heart attack and a seizure. I could not tell you which diseases are
fatal, contagious, or benign. But my lack of knowledge does not
prevent me form investing in penny stocks in the medical field. I
can still invest in those stocks because I can rely on their professional knowledge.

We all know people who can be considered experts in their
fields. They know the ins and outs of their respective fields. They
might be bakers, lawyers, artists, doctors, nutritionists, pilots,
mechanics, travel agents; the list goes on and on. We need to use
the sources of information that we have at our disposal to succeed
in areas we are not familiar with. You would be surprised at the
level of the expertise and information your friends and relatives
have in their fields. I had a great chemistry professor in college
who I could discuss various medicines that drug companies were
developing. Another professor taught me how to be meticulous in
my research and work habits. Their knowledge proved to be invaluable in researching penny stocks.

You can learn a great deal from the people you know. Pretend that they are part of your research department. Instead of hiring an expert to evaluate a company that has developed a new brake system for cars, you can simply run a summary of the penny stock by your family mechanic. If you need a second opinion speak to a car enthusiast and ask him about necessity and viability of the product. If the product and its usefulness impress them you know you are on to something. To summarize, spend time analyzing the sources and degree of knowledge your family and friends represent. Determine what filed you could obtain the best information on based on their expertise. If your family consists mostly of firemen you want to focus on penny stocks dealing with fire departments. Your family will be able to tell you which products a fire department needs and if the penny stock offers a product or service that would be useful to firemen. Since I can assure you that there are few if any analysts following companies catering to fire departments you will be way ahead of the game. You will have your own analyst department catering to researching penny stocks.

These are some of the fields you should look into along with what type of people could help you research them.

Drug Stocks- Doctors, medical professionals, professors.

Internet Stocks- Web site owners, computer programmers, web developers, e-commerce specialists.

Food Stocks- Local supermarket manager, owner of a small food retail shop, chefs.

Entertainment Stocks- Manager's of movie theaters, directors, producers, actors, performers, music promoters.

Oil Stocks- Gas station owners, gasoline distributors, and oil distributors.

Gambling Stocks-Gambling enthusiasts, casino employees, and casino managers.

Travel and Leisure Stocks- Travel agents, frequent travelers, hotel managers, resort managers, and tour guides.

There are many more fields you will be interested in. The objective is to discuss the product or service offered by the penny stock company with the potential end users. A tour guide operator will know what his customers expect and desire on a vacation. The hotel manager knows if there is potential for a new type of hotel, while the gas station owner knows if there is a need for a new type of gas pump. They are must be highly knowledgeable in their fields to be successful. What you are doing is using their high degree of knowledge to ensure your success in selecting penny stocks with the highest degree of potential.

Strategy # 11

Trade high volume penny stocks. High volume stocks offer you the opportunity to buy and sell large amounts of share without influencing the price of the stock. Large orders for a stock with low volume would move the price, making it hard to fill your entire order at the price that you have set your limit at. In contrast, high volume stocks offer enough volume to swallow up any reasonable trade without changing the price. Also as the volume increases for a penny stock more market makers join the action and set their own bid and ask for the stock. The competition between market makers is beneficial to investors since they are competing to buy your shares and sell you shares. The competition between market makers forces the price they are willing to sell you shares at down and the price they are willing to buy your shares at up. They know that if the offer you less than the other market makers for your shares your broker will route your trade to the higher paying market maker. The same process takes place with your buy order; the order goes to the cheapest market maker. A low volume penny stock only has one market maker handling the trading since there is not enough business to convince another market maker to make a market in the stock.

Strategy # 12

You can actively trade penny stocks. You can buy and sell stocks based on short-term events and price fluctuations the way a day trader would day trade established stocks. There are many ways to day trade penny stocks. They are all challenging and require persistence and optimism. You need to be persistent since it will take time to develop your own personal penny stock trading method. The optimism is important to motivate you at the beginning when your first trades do not go the way you wanted them to go. If you do not have a high degree of persistence and optimism you have two choices at this point. Close the book and give up, or go out, buy yourself a motivational book, and develop the optimism and persistence that you have inside.

My favorite form of short-term penny stock trading is based on the daily press releases. I scan the headlines of all the OTC press releases every morning from 9-9:20. I pick out my favorite release for the day and watch the pre-market activity for the stock until 9:30. If I see that the market makers have not brought up the price for the stock I like I will place an order for it. By 10:30 if the press release was as powerful as I expect it to be I sell out my position. I make sure to do this before 10:30 because I have found that the penny stock day traders use the hour between 10:30 and 11:30 to sell their initial holdings. After the selling subsides by 11:30 I come in and buy the stock again waiting for the stock to pick up as more investors read the press release. At this point I can either sell the stock again by 3:00 or hold it until the next day.

Another method is to buy penny stocks in the last 20 minutes of the day when all the day traders are closing their daily positions. You are looking for 10% drops in the price when the day traders exit their positions. You buy the stock and place an order to sell the stock the next morning as soon as the market opens. Penny stocks will most often open up a few percentage points higher than they closed the previous trading day. By selling the stock at 9:35 you have tried to capture the previous day's last minute 10%

drop in price and today's 3% increase in price. That's 13% in two days and you still have the rest of the day to continue trading.

We have already discussed the dip strategy in which you buy a stock after it has dropped and now has started to recover. If you have the drive you can practice the dip strategy through out the day. You can look for stocks that have experienced a sharp increase at the beginning of the day and now are being sold off. When the stock starts stabilizing you can call in an order and try to buy it for a cent or two below the current price. If you catch it at your limit price you can then place another order and sell the stock for 5% more than you bought it for. This strategy differentiates from the other dip strategy in that we do not wait for it to start heading back up since all we want to do is make a quick profit whenever the stock rebounds that day. The stock might end the day at a lower price than you bought it for which is fine, as long as you were able to sell it for a few percentage points more than you bought it for. If you follow this strategy and see that the stock continues falling after having stabilized you call in another order to sell your shares.

Momentum plays require you to be very quick and steadfast. When a stock is promoted by a newsletter or investment recommendation service you can buy the stock as soon as the day opens, call back and place an order to sell the stock for 10% more than you bought it for and watch the price very closely after to make sure you are able to get out before the price comes back down. Remember that the reason the stock is promoted is to allow someone to sell his or her holdings in to the market. You are going to have to sell out before this individual sells his or her position. Set a price that you are comfortable buying the stock for and the minimum price you are willing to sell the stock for. Once you have set the price you are willing to buy the stock at stick to it or you will find yourself chasing the price, which can start dropping any minute. The same on the sell side, just because you feel that you can get more for the stock do not become tempted to increase your limit sell order or you will find that sooner or later you will set it too high and have to resort to selling at a loss when the price drops.

Strategy # 13

Limit your loss to 20% on any penny stock. Once your penny stock drops 20% below the price you bought it at sell the stock. If it has dropped below 20% it will continue dropping even further because of all the investors who are either going to choose to take out their profits or cut their losses. If you really like the stock, you can always buy the stock a few days later at a much cheaper price. And if you are waiting for the stock to rebound you are better off in a stock that has not experienced a significant price change yet. The stock that has dropped more than 20% will have a certain stigma for at least a few days and investors will not buy it. The stock that is only starting to attract attention does not have any barriers to increasing by more than 20%.

CONCLUSION

Investing and trading in penny stocks is potentially highly rewarding but also tremendously risky. The purpose of this book is not to recommend penny stock investing or trading to anyone. The book is written for people who have already decided that they want to invest and trade penny stocks. The book is meant to educate those people who have already made the decisions. I also would like to convey that investors should make their own decisions and realize that I am not an investment advisor nor am I giving investment advice. This book is not written in any advisor capacity. The book is meant only as an educational book. I have made and lost huge amounts of money in penny stocks. When I first started investing in penny stocks three years ago I lost 80% of all the money in my account within the year. You might not be so lucky.

If you still want to invest in and trade penny stocks you should start out with a small amount that you could afford to lose. This way if you lose the money you will not suffer. And if you do find a real winner, your investment should still be able to grow significantly.

You should discuss anything you read in this book with an investment advisor before you act on it.

Okay, now that I have scared you and made you regret getting exited about penny stocks in the first place let me leave you with some optimistic words. You can be successful at anything if you put your heart into it and work hard. You need to persevere even when it is difficult and the road seems to be too much of a challenge for you. I believe that penny stocks, like other financial and business ventures, require an enormous effort and hard work. I also believe that the hard work and effort will pay off to those who commit themselves to being successful.

I have one final note. The year that I lost 80% of my account was followed by a 1000% gain in my account without putting a single additional dollar in my account. G-d's help and hard work pays off.